ONLY TO SERVE

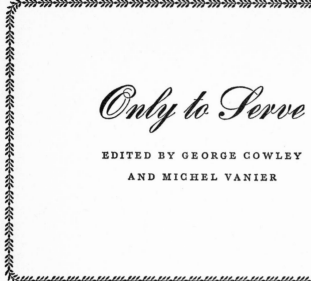

Only to Serve

EDITED BY GEORGE COWLEY
AND MICHEL VANIER

UNIVERSITY OF TORONTO PRESS

SELECTIONS FROM ADDRESSES OF
GOVERNOR-GENERAL

Georges P. Vanier

© University of Toronto Press 1970
Printed in Canada by
University of Toronto Press
Toronto and Buffalo
ISBN 0-8020-1573-5

PHOTO CREDITS
In order of appearance:
Photo Features Limited
Canadian Forces Photo
Gazette Photo Service
Montreal Star/Canada Wide
Montreal Star/Canada Wide
Mme Georges P. Vanier
Gazette Photo Service
CP Wirephoto
Montreal Star/Canada Wide
Donald McKague, Toronto
CP Wirephoto

Contents

Foreword

CLAUDE RYAN

THE POSITION OF GOVERNOR-GENERAL IS, AT FIRST GLANCE, A DIFFICULT AND unattractive one. He appears to be the very incarnation of authority, and yet he possesses no authority in his own right, and can exercise even less. His actions are dictated in advance by the all-encompassing demands of rules and precedent, which form a protocol so strict that it leaves hardly the tiniest room, at least on the surface, for personal initiative. The governor-general occupies the summit of the whole political structure of our country, yet he must refrain from the least act or statement which could be interpreted as interference in a domain which belongs to those who hold the actual reins of power. His approval must be obtained before any important decision becomes law, but he has not one whit to say in the way such decisions are reached. Presiding, as it were, over the entire functioning of the political system, he must feel at times that he is in reality the system's most minor and ineffectual servant. His name comes first on every official list, but in the day-to-day life of his nation it is often forgotten altogether.

Having spent a considerable time on the staffs of governors-general,

Georges P. Vanier was more aware than most of both the grandeur and the limitations that come with the vice-regal office when he himself was offered the post in succession to Vincent Massey in 1959. If he accepted the position in spite of the fact that he was already seventy years old, he did so simply because he wanted to go on serving his country, as he had done throughout his life in the most varied capacities. But so far did this man carry the ideal of service that, without ever having sought to do so, he conferred upon the position of governor-general a moral stature which it had never before attained. His extraordinary achievements in this respect long remained hidden from the eyes of casual observers. Their full splendour broke forth only at the time of Mr. Vanier's death. Their magnitude could be attributed, we believe, to the fact that his actions as governor-general were entirely removed from politics; what they lost in the renunciation of material power they more than made up for in moral and spiritual influence.

The years which marked Mr. Vanier's sojourn at Rideau Hall are remembered as turbulent ones. From 1962 to 1967, the country was led by minority governments. The rise of Quebec nationalism created such strained relations between Ottawa and Quebec that it seemed to place the whole future of Canada in doubt. The country's economy was shaken by continuous buffeting. Parliament itself became a theatre of crises, crises which were often a disgrace. Only history will be able to determine with precision the exact role the governor-general played during these difficult years. But it is interesting to note that never throughout the entire period did the least breath of intrigue or rumour of misuse of influence circulate concerning the Governor-General's person. A lesser man than Mr. Vanier, and history has shown us enough of them, would perhaps have been tempted to profit from the vacuum which paralysed the functioning of the legislative and executive process to look for ways to extend his own sphere of influence. At the very least he would have succumbed at one time or other to the temptations to express, if only by one of those indiscretions which men in public life know the secret of using so well, some note of justifiable irritation or impatience with the abuses which public opinion were rebelling against. Never, however, could one accuse Mr. Vanier of giving in to any such temptation. He was at all times the governor-general. No matter how urgent the crisis, he would carefully consult the most reputable experts in parliamentary procedure, the better to be ready for every eventuality. He never looked for the least opportunity, even when one seemed ready-made, to step beyond his role. He would have defended the vice-regal position against every effort to diminish it or to reduce it to insignificance, but it would never have occurred to him to try to expand his power at the expense of parliamentary principles. The men of politics, both the leaders and the ordinary members of Parliament, respected and loved Mr. Vanier profoundly. He in turn always maintained and freely admitted to a respect no less profound for their own distinct roles.

If it was not his place to intervene in the daily unfolding of primarily political activity, Mr. Vanier felt nonetheless a duty in his capacity as governor-general to establish special bonds directly with the Canadian people. A governor-general is pictured in certain circles as a sort of moral hostage, who is allowed to occupy the keystone position in the ruling hierarchy on condition that he limit his role to one of passive endorsement of other people's decisions. This was not the interpretation which Mr. Vanier had of his duties, nor was it the interpretation which emerged from his words and actions as governor-general. Mr. Vanier saw himself in such an office as one whose primary mission was to be in close rapport with every aspect of Canadian life, official or private, modest or grandiose. From 1959 to 1967, Rideau Hall was not, as it had been in other eras, the whirling centre of the fashionable life. High society receptions and formal balls were relatively rare. On the other hand, the Governor-General's house served continuously as a meeting place where the vice-regal couple (for Madame Vanier was also always and admirably present) could welcome representatives of the most diverse sectors of Canadian society.

Mr. Vanier took a lively interest in politics, in economics, in military life, in arts and letters, in social welfare, in religion. He had a particular concern for the poor and the humble, for youth, and for the family. He loved to meet Canadians in their own home surroundings and to see them at work in their habitual environments and he loved equally to receive at Rideau Hall persons from every walk of life. During these innumerable encounters, which characterized his tour of duty, Mr. Vanier's primary concern was never to draw attention to the prerogatives of his office or to the titles that encumbered him. He was able to separate from these trappings a genuine interest in the individual personalities of his guests or hosts, a sincere and humble wish to become better informed about the many activities indulged in by a people whom he continuously wished to know better. Equally at ease, as was his wife, in the company of a head of state or of a group of municipal aldermen or chief scouts, he always managed to create the impression that he was present simply to provide the other person with a chance to express himself. Had one not known him, one might have assumed that a governor-general would act as if he were the incarnation of power and splendour, sitting on a high throne and receiving the obeissance of the subjects of his kingdom. Mr. Vanier was totally different. He was a man who embodied the spirit of hospitality, a man eager to hear whatever truth his visitors or his hosts could bring to him.

Mr. Vanier was called upon, it goes without saying, to speak frequently. He made it his duty to begin each encounter by listening, as much as possible, but he was too much aware of the responsibilities of his office not to know that when he visited somewhere he could be expected to speak. The occasions during his tour of duty when he was invited to speak were innumerable. Perhaps never from any other Canadian in public life came words which attained so high a degree of unassuming simplicity or, more accurately, of spirituality.

Mr. Vanier was not an eloquent man. He was probably too sincere to try resorting to that artificiality of speech which public men so often abuse. But he must surely have taken considerable care in drafting his speeches, because to those who knew him well his words expressed perfectly what he thought. It seems certain that in editing his messages he set his sights on the goal of giving to Canadian public life a sort of supplement for its soul, an infusion of a high patriotism, even of pure and simple spirituality; these were qualities which people had long since given up expecting to find in partisan politicians. People sustain themselves and progress by means of the laws and institutions which they fashion for themselves. But institutions and laws are rendered virtually ineffective if they do not rest in the last analysis on individual conscience, on a quality of spirit, on a framework of moral values shared and served in common.

To make clear to the Canadian people these moral and spiritual depths upon which their past history and their future are founded; to express a concept of patriotism which rises above partisan or racist, overt or covert sectarianism; to establish a harmonious link between the call of the spirit and the temporal destinies of these people whom he loved: such was, it would seem to us, the inspiration which governed the writing of General Vanier's public speeches and messages in the performance of his duties as governor-general.

Mr. Vanier was manifestly receptive to every form of human progress, as, for example, his interest in the development of universities and scientific research well illustrates. On questions of public life and the progress of civilization, he had lofty views which drew from the purest well-springs of the great philosophical traditions of the West. But he was at the same time and to a very rare degree a profoundly religious man; one of the most moving aspects of his sojourn at Rideau Hall was without doubt the royal liberty which he granted himself at every circumstance to bear witness to his faith in God. In an environment where by weakness more than by malice one tends to confine all too willingly one's religious values to one's private life alone, Mr. Vanier never hesitated to testify frankly and publicly to his convictions. Never, however, did he do so in a way designed to hurt other people. He spoke of what he saw with the eyes of a believer because he respected his enquirers too much to hide from them his own vision of the world. But he knew as well that others saw things differently. Any denial of God, however it expressed itself, caused him deep pain, but he never allowed himself to judge others who did not think as he did.

Above everything there was in this man a quality which we have rarely found in the same degree of perfection in any other man in the public eye. That quality was love. Wherever he found himself, in the military life, in diplomacy, in political life, Mr. Vanier loved others very much indeed. He loved his compatriots whether of French, English, or any other background. He loved his own people and he loved those other people whom his duties led him to know. He loved those whom he was called upon to obey and those whom his lot fell to command. He loved with special affection the poor, the humble, children, and the fathers and mothers of families. He loved the members of his own family. He loved with the same love every morally admissible form of human activity. He loved men and all things of God, and God himself, because it was God who was at the source of everything he did. It was God with whom he spent long periods in communion every day and to whom he felt himself to be returning, a further step each day, with the joyful serenity of a child.

This man was a good man. He has left to his country a testimony of peace. The speeches and the messages which we read in this collection describe him better than anything else could. We may find on each page the imprint of great human wisdom as well as of spiritual clarity, to a degree given only to those who live in the love of God and of their neighbour.

Montreal
June 1968

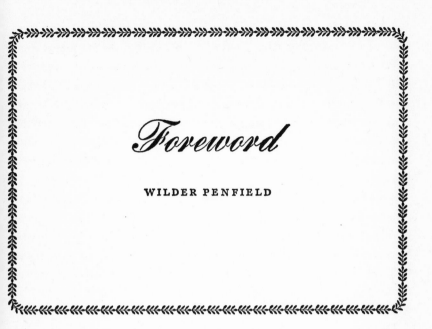

Foreword

WILDER PENFIELD

GEORGES PHILIAS VANIER, DISTINGUISHED SOLDIER AND DIPLOMAT, HAS A unique place in the hearts of his countrymen. As governor-general, he became a symbol of their own strength and integrity. When he died, on 5 March 1967, they mourned for him as men had mourned at the passing of Winston Churchill.

These two great men were very different, the one British, the other altogether Canadian. But each will live on as a leader of thought while the story of his life and the causes for which he strove will be his enduring memorial. Each will continue to speak to posterity through his talks and writings.

Georges Vanier was a French Canadian. From the start, he was easily bilingual, since his parents had been wise enough to let him hear some English spoken as well as French in the crucial years before the age of six. As the years passed, he wanted to be known as a Canadian. He understood and valued without prejudice those varied cultures, old and new, which make our country what it is.

Georges P. Vanier, the son of Montreal businessman Philias Vanier, was born on 23 April 1888. After study at Loyola College, he graduated from Laval University in Montreal and began the practice of law in Montreal. With the advent of war in 1914, he left his office to help organize Canada's first French-Canadian volunteer unit, which was to become the Vingt-deuxième Régiment, more famous among English-speaking comrades as the "Vandoos." He served with them, was twice wounded, and in the end, losing a leg by amputation at mid-thigh, he was discharged and entered a law firm.

But soon, after reconsidering careers, he went to Army Headquarters again, walking on his artificial leg, and offered to enlist. The officer-in-charge laughed, well-meaning but unkind, and said, "No." "I thought," Vanier explained, "you might have use for brains in the Canadian Army as well as legs." He returned to the practice of law until a belated, but very enthusiastic, invitation arrived. Would he accept a commission in the Army? He did, and thus he became a professional soldier.

The war was over now, and he had made another proposal – he would have called it the most important proposal in his career – to a French-Canadian girl from Montreal, Pauline Archer. She did not refuse.

He was posted for a year as aide-de-camp to Lord Byng, who was then governor-general in Ottawa. After that he rose rapidly in rank, until he was made commander of the Vingt-deuxième Régiment. Before long, however, he was invited to embark on a diplomatic career. He hesitated, but finally agreed with the provision that he could preserve his standing in the Canadian Army.

So he served in the Department of External Affairs, at the League of Nations in Geneva, and on various commissions. From 1931 to 1939, he was secretary to the Office of the High Commissioner for Canada in London. There he was junior to Howard Ferguson and later Vincent Massey, who was destined to precede him as governor-general. He was also an associate of Lester B. Pearson, one day to be prime minister.

During the Second World War and in the difficult days that followed it, he served as minister and later ambassador to France, fifteen years in all. Over this period, he came to understand and to admire the people of France. He wrote a book, *Paroles de guerre – Un Canadien parle aux Français*.

When the Vaniers returned to Canada and subsequently to Ottawa and Government House, they made every effort to study the Canadian scene and its social problems, seeing it, as they were able to do, in broad perspective. But, to understand the present was not enough for him. Like a prophet of old, it was his purpose, as he said, to see "beyond the horizon of our time."

Soon he set on foot a Canadian Conference on the Family. It was held at Rideau Hall in the spring of 1964 and there I heard him speak. "Change has brought a crisis on the family," he began. This was common knowledge to all thoughtful men in the postwar West. But General Vanier went a step further. He issued a challenge. "The future is in our hands," he said, "It is up to us to direct the course of civilization."

What a challenge that was! After the conference, a group of men and women took counsel with him. They planned a series of discussions. During the year that followed, they met from time to time at Government House. Gradually a unique institution was visualized and a constitution written. In the spring of 1965, a charter was granted establishing *The Vanier Institute of the Family/l'Institut Vanier de la famille*. Its objective was, and is, to study all aspects of the family in a changing world, and to take action for its enrichment and for the betterment of human society. The action is not in the field of "family welfare" or in that of religion, but in an allied field of study, communication and home-education.

Since the death of Georges Vanier, the Institute has begun to operate, as he hoped it would, with income from a gradually increasing endowment. This is the people's tribute to a great Canadian.

But, from a realistic point of view, the Vanier Institute is a unique idea and a practical movement that will grow. It is the gift this man and his wife wished to leave to the people of Canada.

Beyond that, the Governor-General left behind him another priceless heritage – the memory of a man and the inspiration of a spirit that will go with us into the future. His approaches to life were varied. Deeply religious, he had the perceptions of a mystic, but always balanced by a broad-minded appreciation of other human philosophies. He was a genial, kindly host, a faithful friend, and a vivid companion. He was given to unpredictable flashes of merriment, especially when in company with the very young.

Even his wife could never be sure just when a puckish impulse would cause him to elaborate some almost plausible fabrication intended to tease her. In the spring of 1966, she was, herself, granted honorary diplomas from several Canadian universities. Last of all came a degree, *honoris causa,* from McGill University. The Governor-General was officially "Visitor" of that university, and he attended the ceremony. During the governors' luncheon which followed, he was asked to say a few words quite off the public record. "Well," he said, "of course I don't want to be misunderstood. But I have noticed a recently changing attitude on the part of the public press. When my wife received one of her previous degrees, our pictures appeared in a newspaper. The caption read, 'Madame Vanier honoured. The man on her right is prominent in public affairs.'" The other guests at the luncheon saw an expression of astonishment on his wife's face. She leaned forward to look at her husband. He was apparently dead serious. Then he added: "This morning a Montreal newspaper pictured us, and the legend read, 'The man with Madame Vanier has not yet been identified!'"

On the eve of Canada's centennial celebration, there were danger signals. His heart was failing, it seemed. But events of great moment loomed before him and before his companion of many years, Lester B. Pearson, now prime minister. Cross-currents in political affairs seemed to threaten unity and the destiny of his country. He could not turn away from any challenge. He would carry on, he said, "as long as God gives me strength."

On New Year's Day, his voice was as strong and vibrant as ever when he spoke to a country-wide audience: "The resolution which the Canadian nation must now propose for 1967 and the century to come is the unity of our country. The road to unity is the road of love."

As the first weeks of the new year passed, he was losing ground but he worked on with an air of impatient gaiety. Driving vigour and courage rose within him like sap in a young tree. "People do not really age by merely living a number of years," he said. "I am convinced that we grow old only by deserting our ideals. We are as old as our faith and our hope, especially faith and hope in our youth."

Three days before the end, he spoke to a group of undergraduates from the University of Montreal. They had come to Government House and he welcomed them, sitting in his wheelchair. He was panting a little and his cheeks were flushed for he had reached the stage when he needed to breathe oxygen. He held his rugged head high and made what was to be his last public address. It closed with these words:

Do not think me a pessimist. One often hears the cries of distress of those who long for what they call "the good old times," but I tell you the good times are now. The best time is always the present time, because it alone offers the opportunity for action, because it is ours, because on God's scale, it is apocalyptic, a time when the lines between good and evil are clearly drawn, and each of us must choose his side, a time when there is no longer room for either the coward or the uncommitted.

A Canadian hero has passed from us, confident that we will direct the course of our civilization. He will speak to us again and again in the years to come when we stop and listen and read what he wrote.

Sussex House
Austin, Quebec
August 1968

Preface

GOVERNOR-GENERAL VANIER WOULD HAVE BEEN THE LAST TO ENCOURAGE this publication of extracts from his speeches. He delighted in making fun of himself in general, and of his speech-making abilities in particular. "My most attentive audience," he once declared solemnly, "was on an occasion when a sudden rainstorm forced us all indoors. I talked on at shameless length, until I suddenly realized that I had been holding forth for over half an hour. 'I am afraid I have kept you too long,' I said to my audience. 'Oh no, Sir,' said a spokesman from the back of the hall, 'please go on, it's still raining!' "

"There is a feeling in public circles," he noted half seriously, "which has grown almost into a legend, that the Governor-General is able, willing, and possibly anxious to let off steam on every available occasion. I am doing my best to slay this dragon that lies in wait for me!" But the dragon persisted: he was asked and agreed to speak formally on nearly six hundred occasions as governor-general. He was called upon to make impromptu speeches as many times again, and sent, in answer to requests, nearly one thousand written messages.

From this vast record of his spoken and written words, we have had the happy but impossible task of trying to choose those excerpts which would most nearly do justice to the broad range of his interests, and the profound depth of his compassion. We will, we fear, have omitted many passages which others will remember and look for in vain. We have also felt obliged to confine ourselves to an examination of those speeches and messages General Vanier delivered while actually serving as governor-general. Jean Vanier has included some of his father's talks given prior to 1958, particularly those of a religious nature, in his book *In Weakness, Strength*, and Robert Speaight will quote a number of passages from other pre-1958 speeches in a forthcoming biography.

The Governor-General would also have been the last to lay claim to any absolutes of originality in his point of view and references. If some of the material in the excerpts we have chosen should, therefore, more properly be credited to other sources, we ask the authors' forgiveness. General Vanier had a remarkable memory for a telling phrase or a useful illustration, and in using them, he was careful to disclaim any pride of authorship, seeking simply the enjoyment or the inspiration of his listeners. Nonetheless, somehow the words he spoke became uniquely his own, for the grace and strength of his delivery, the warmth of his feeling, and the patent sincerity of his convictions were the qualities that really imbued his words with meaning and relevance long after their time of delivery.

May we take this opportunity to record our gratitude to Dr. Wilder Penfield and to Claude Ryan, who so generously contributed forewords to this book; to the Canada Council, for its indispensable support and encouragement; to the University of Ottawa, which administered the Canada Council grant; to the University of Toronto Press, which gave us invaluable editorial help; to the National Library, which provided office space and research assistance; and to Mme. Laurette Chateauvert, who so patiently and cheerfully sifted with us the millions of words from which we have presumed to choose these extracts.

George Cowley
Michel Vanier

ONLY TO SERVE

Inaugural Address

Reply of His Excellency the Governor-General to the address of the Prime Minister in the Senate Chamber on the day of His Excellency's installation as Governor-General of Canada, 15 September 1959

MR. PRIME MINISTER, MY FIRST WORDS ARE A PRAYER. MAY ALMIGHTY GOD in his infinite wisdom and mercy bless the sacred mission which has been entrusted to me by Her Majesty the Queen and help me to fulfil it in all humility. In exchange for his strength, I offer him my weakness. May he give peace to this beloved land of ours and, to those who live in it, the grace of mutual understanding, respect and love.

I shall have the honour to convey to Her Majesty the message of devotion and loyalty to which you have given expression on behalf of the people of Canada. The recent visit of our Sovereign to this country, with His Royal Highness the Duke of Edinburgh, has made of the word loyalty a synonym of affection. The Queen has established with Canadians a bond personal rather than formal. Aptly does Shakespeare evoke this feeling in Henry vi:

"My crown is in my heart, not on my head." Is it surprising that such a crown should find its way into our hearts as well?

We are deeply grateful, my wife and I, for the generous terms and the charming way in which you have welcomed us.

I am happy to pay tribute to my predecessor, the first Canadian governor-general. He had to blaze a new trail and well has he done it. During seven and a half years, never sparing himself, he has laboured with fortitude and devotion in the service of his Sovereign and his country. His place is very high in the list of those who have had the honour to represent the Crown in Canada. From the bottom of my heart I thank him for the assistance and advice he has given me. I have no illusions about being able to equal his achievement.

We are indeed fortunate in being attached to the Crown which holds for the world a promise of peace. It is well to recall that the Queen is the symbol of the free association of member nations of the Commonwealth and as such is accepted as its head. The total area of the Commonwealth is estimated to be about fourteen and a half million square miles and its population something in the neighbourhood of six hundred and fifty millions.

Canada forms part of this mighty far-flung Commonwealth, which is composed of many races and creeds. What a power is there for good in the world, what a power to right many wrongs, to solve many problems, in amity, without recourse to arms! Does not the very thought of the Commonwealth's potential action conjure up a vision inspiring in scope and grandeur?

You have drawn attention, Mr. Prime Minister, to the significance of this day. How right you are. Two hundred years ago, a certain country won a battle on the Plains of Abraham; another country lost a battle. In the annals of every nation, there is a record of victories and defeats. The present Sovereign of the victorious country, Sovereign also of Canada now, returns to the same battle-field, two centuries later, and presents colours to a French-speaking regiment, which mounts guard over the Citadel of Quebec, a regiment of which Her Majesty is colonel-in-chief.

And how is the battle of 1759 commemorated? By a monument, erected in 1828, to the memory of both commanding generals, who died in action. It bears the inscription in Latin: "Valour gave them a common death, history a common fame, posterity a common monument." Is there a better way to heal the wounds of war, to seal the bonds of peace?

The sixty thousand French Canadians of 1759 have become several millions. For two thousand years, more or less, the annals of history proclaim the fame and glory of Great Britain and France. The future of Canada is linked with this double fabulous heritage. Canadians of Anglo-Saxon and French descent, whose two cultures will always be a source of mutual enrichment, are an inspiring example of coexistence. They go forward hand in hand to make Canada a great nation, hand in hand also with Canadians of every origin, with their heritages, irrespective of race or creed. We are all God's children.

Each one of us, in his own way and place, however humble, must play his part towards the fulfilment of our national destiny. To realize how mighty this destiny will be, let us lift our eyes beyond the horizon of our time. In our march forward in material happiness, let us not neglect the spiritual threads in the weaving of our lives. If Canada is to attain the greatness worthy of it, each of us must say, "I ask only to serve."

The Family

THE FAMILY OFFERS TO MAN THE POSSIBILITY OF FINDING THE GREATEST happiness available on earth. Certainly up to the present no one has discovered any substitute that can replace the family. Wise men tell us that if through some stroke of misfortune the family were eliminated, we would have to provide a separate psychiatrist to take care of each child.

It is, after all, the family which fulfils the need of each one of us to love and to be loved. In the interplay of responsibility and dependence within the family are also found the well-springs of love, love for God, for one's religion, and for one's country. Within the family the sense of value of the individual can develop. Perhaps you have heard the story of the testimony made by the mother of a boy who had been hailed before a court of law. When she was asked what sort of child he was, she replied: "He's a fine boy, Your Honour. It's just what he *does* that is wrong." Little wonder from this story how the family can provide an atmosphere of reconciliation and how its members never cease to love each other, even when they sin.

Not only does the family provide the creative forces which fashion the finer aspects of a child's personality, but it inspires as well the first realizations of responsibility to others. The essence of life led together by parents and children is sharing. All members of the family partake of each other's joys and sorrows, each other's love and suffering. In this sharing, selfishness slowly dies away, and one becomes able to give oneself in the service of others.

Since the family is also a miniature version of society as a whole, the qualities which make for good relations between members of the family also make of them good citizens of the larger community. What future would the community have if its members thought only of themselves and refused to help each other? Society must have citizens with open hearts, able to dedicate themselves to the common good, and such citizens will be found first and foremost among members of families where the spirit of generosity and service has taken root.

We are all painfully aware of the rise of social delinquency in our own country during the present time, and I am told that Canada is among those nations which have the highest incidence of alcoholism. Certain of our cities already have a tragic reputation for their rates of crime in general. The morality of our youth often leaves much to be desired, and the number of broken homes continues to increase. Surely it is time that society made a conscientious examination of itself. Should we place the power of selfishness and pride before that of generosity and service? Where will our present course take us? Have we the will to seek and establish a better life, or are we simply interested in the quest for more material possessions?

To face these problems which I have outlined, to overcome them, and to guide our steps towards national maturity, we must first of all ensure that family life is based on firm foundations. Nothing less than this assurance will do. Only the family, through the intimacy of the training it can provide, is in a position to counterbalance the temptations to do wrong. If parents fulfil their responsibilities, this training will be started at the youngest possible age, even before the full development of a child's reasoning powers, and such training in the end creates young people who are spiritually mature and firmly grounded in morality.

Unfortunately, strong forces have already weakened and are continuing to menace the integrity of family life. It used to be that in smaller communities where everybody knew each other, the force of public opinion influenced individual behaviour. Nowadays, however, our larger cities are more and more composed of persons without any real roots in the community. A survey conducted in Saskatoon, for example, revealed that only six per cent of those polled had been born in that city. The atmosphere of permanency and stability in social relations is disappearing, and with it the larger family circle, which once comprised three generations and included aunts, uncles, and cousins, is also disappearing. Nowadays the normal family circle consists only of mother, father, and children. At the very time when there is a greater need than ever before for breadth and strength in the family, the fortress is being stripped of most of its former buttresses.

Family unity is threatened by certain ideas which have arisen out of reaction to the rigidity prevalent in the nineteenth century. In times past, a marriage was often arranged primarily to give expression to an agreement or alliance between two families. Nowadays, however, the more romantic concept of marriage as a free choice has seized the public's imagination. More than that, novels, films, and television today suggest that falling in love is not only the sole justification but also the sole preparation needed for marriage. The life of a married couple is portrayed as a euphoria of love and happiness, instead of as a profound matter of fidelity between two persons, and as a first step towards procreation and the upbringing of children.

This emphasis on total liberty in marriage instead of on the actual requirements of mutual dependence leads inevitably to divorce. A marriage which is made only with the object of satisfying the personal desires of the two participants is doomed to failure when this personal satisfaction is diminished or frustrated. Between 1941 and 1951 the number of divorces in Canada doubled. One need hardly be surprised that delinquency, prostitution, alcoholism, drug addiction, and other moral ills pose as many problems as they do. These evils very often find their origin in the degeneration of the family, to be passed on to and multiplied in subsequent generations.

The libertine concept within the family results in the exaggerated independence all too often accorded to our youth. Self-centred parents have neither the time nor the will to instruct and supervise their children. The same greed for libertine indulgence and purely selfish happiness has resulted in a reluctance to have children at all. Such reluctance makes the union between the married couple precarious, and severe restrictions in the number of children in the family deprive both children and parents of those precious elements of mutual understanding and affection which the members of larger families are able to give to each other.

I have tried to outline certain concepts which have arisen in reaction to the past, and which our present century has tended to accept without reservation, but it is not only these abstract concepts and the results of their application which threaten family integrity. There is also an economic aspect to the problem. The number of working married women tripled between 1941 and 1951 in Canada. At the end of that decade fully eleven per cent of married women were working outside of their homes. Today the figure is closer to nineteen per cent. Of course, many of these working married women have no children, and many as well work only for a part of the week, but when both father and mother are working, the risk arises that the ability to distinguish between what is necessary to life and what is a mere luxury will become blurred, and certain fundamental family values will be sacrificed. While this problem is most serious when very young children are involved, it is also a threat to the welfare of those who are attending school, and who find no one dear to them to welcome them when they return home each day from class. Surely a mother should contemplate working outside of the home only under exceptional circumstances, and then for only the most imperative reasons.

We often say that our age is an age of progress. It is certainly one which has produced rapid changes. The far-reaching effects of these changes require great powers of adaptation by parents, parents who have of course formed their own attitudes and ways of thinking in a previous period. Without this adaptability, understanding between parents and children is bound to be difficult. We must be on our guard continuously against any tendency towards intolerance or indifference on the part of either parents or children. Parents must act with prudence and wisdom and confine their condemnation only to that which is morally reprehensible.

Let us consider for a moment how we can defend, improve, and deepen family life to make it more adaptable to the requirements of our age.

We need a concept of marriage based on faithfulness and on a recogni-

9

tion of permanence. Real love is a gift and not a loan. Marriage is more than a mere legal contract which one can make or unmake at will. If we can succeed in making the true nature of marriage understood, we will be able thereby to eradicate many of the ills which at present beset the structure of our society. It seems to me that one of the best ways to enhance this understanding is by means of marriage preparation courses. Such courses cover not only the religious aspects of marriage but the whole field of married life.

On the economic plane we should try to establish the mother's position in the home on a solid foundation. Setting up a family budget is the first step. Surveys made at Sault Ste. Marie and Saskatoon reveal that only one family in three regularly draws up a budget. One of the conclusions reached at a congress on our life in society held at Banff was to the effect that it was not lack of income which caused the greatest economic difficulties in family life, but rather wastage which arose from poor administration of existing economic resources. A married couple must sit down and plan the best allocation of their resources together. Only thus can they avoid falling victim to crippling debts and assure a sound future for their family within the means at their disposal.

Great efforts must still be made in the field of parental education. Parents must have a profound understanding of the factors which affect the development of a child's character and personality. They must be fully aware of their responsibility, for example, in directing the child's leisure activities. Such responsibilities will necessarily require close contact with the child's school authorities. At present much too large a proportion of students abandon their education and "drop out" before having completed even their elementary schooling. The encouragement and support of parents are indispensable in lowering this high proportion of "drop-outs," the existence of which is making infinitely more difficult the task of forming a younger generation sufficiently mature and qualified to create its own families and bring up a subsequent generation in its turn.

I have tried to use reasons drawn from nature in emphasizing the importance of the role the family plays in moral considerations which affect all of humankind. The means of satisfying our basic instincts for our own preservation, for the establishment of relations with our fellows, and for the reproduction of our species: these means human reason can find only in viable and consecrated life within a family.

At the Club Richelieu Luncheon, Ottawa-Hull, 22 February 1961

(translation)

AS I AM SURE MANY OF YOU KNOW, I HAVE A PARTICULAR INTEREST IN THE role of the family in society, and it was this interest which led my wife and myself to convene, this coming June, a Canadian Conference on the Family ...

[What essential characteristics should distinguish a family?] To begin with, it should be united. It should be fruitful, and it should be dedicated in its service to the living faith of God and to the most noble of our human traditions.

The family should be one in unity, a centre of peace and love. A society composed of profoundly united families will be, I suggest, a profoundly happy society. But this unity of the family is no self-centred clannishness, where the different members turn in on each other, where they close themselves to outsiders, and where their pleasure is derived at the expense of others. On the contrary, the family unit, far from being self-centred, should be a source of generosity and enrichment for others. A united home will instil in its children a selfless spirit, inspiring them to show by their words and examples the unity and the serenity which they have known in their family. They will not go out into the world to grasp, but to give, to devote themselves to the welfare of those less fortunate than themselves – the poor, the sick, those who mourn, or those who suffer from any other of life's ills.

This spirit of generosity seeks to give, not in any sense of paternalism, but out of feelings of genuine love, feelings which inspire the giver to share the suffering as well as the joys of others. If our own good fortune, which after all is a gift to us from God and from nature, is not put to the service of others through love, our consciences will condemn us. We are all, in fact, our brothers' keepers for as long as poverty exists in this world. By 'poverty' I mean not only material poverty, but also spiritual, intellectual, cultural, and psychological poverty, and even the poverty of physical handicaps: these forms of poverty will always be with us. Our sense of generosity must inspire us not only to identify with known individuals and their suffering, but also to seek to create national and even international institutions which can help to supply more general remedies. Only thus can we hope to build a society where each person may find fulfilment in love of God and of his neighbour.

There is one sure way to give expression to this spirit of generosity and to radiate to others the happiness which we ourselves possess. It is not uniquely or even primarily by giving money. It is first and foremost by giving our hearts. Those who are miserable and those who suffer have more often need of affection and friendship than they have need for money. In these days when so many people know the pain of loneliness, especially perhaps in our larger cities, our united and happy homes must be large enough and generous enough to open their hearts and their doors to those in need.

Let us give all our strength to this quest for unity, generosity, faith and loyalty. Let us first seek faith, faith in God above everything, faith in Christ and in his Church; and loyalty to our religious, moral, and cultural heritage. Let us show our faith not only with our lips but with our hearts and minds as well. Let us be loyal not so much to the traditions of our past as to their spirit, for only thus can our faith be open to the inspiration of the present and directed to the promise of the future ...

... Let us never be afraid to remind the world that standing above purely economic, material, or psychological values, there are human values, values of the heart, moral and spiritual values, values that find their source and their strength in the intimacy of a united family where peace and love reign supreme.

You will understand now why my wife and I have called this Conference on the Family. But let me say at once that a gathering of this type cannot produce any instant solutions or immediate remedies to the problems of our age. It may well be that the requirements of our modern world and of our present society mean that some of the factors which helped to keep our families united in the past are now tending to diminish and disappear. The difficulties of family financing, of accommodation, and of contemporary working conditions must inevitably have an influence upon the community as a whole and even more upon the community in miniature which is the family. They must also inevitably sow the seeds of disintegration of the unity of that family.

Our conference will, I hope, undertake an earnest study of every aspect of family life. It will attempt to lay bare those factors which tend to divide the family. It will try to put us on guard against certain doctrines of our day, the effect of which, whether intentionally or not, is to destroy the family in the name of strengthening the state. By seeking a consensus of conscience among men and women in responsible positions, our conference will try to discover how the family can reunite itself and find fulfilment in spite of the problems and complexities of modern life. Finally, the conference will examine and make better known the efforts already being made in Canada to meet these same objectives.

But the task of unifying the family is not something which can be imposed upon us from outside. It is up to each one of us individually, in the privacy of reflection, to examine our consciences and to discover how we can become more understanding and more generous in spirit. By trying, first, in all humility, to change our own hearts and our own attitudes we will best be able to help the family, our country, and all mankind.

At a banquet given by the Fondation de la famille terrienne, Montreal,
8 February 1964 (translation)

I KNOW YOU WILL WISH TO OPEN THIS CONFERENCE BY A PRAYER TO GOD, our common Father, to him who has promised to inspire and to sustain all men of good faith, who try in their respective spheres to love and help their brothers. Is it not the profound meaning of this religious ceremony, of this common prayer, that reunites us in the presence of God, in the same thought, in the same humble and confiding invocation, in the same hope?

It is a great pleasure for me to greet all of you today, you who come from all corners of our vast country for three days of study and work. I thank you for having heeded our appeal.

Throughout the world the little community that is known as the family is passing through a series of crises resulting from certain profound changes in modern man's way of life.

In the early history of mankind there were epochs in which the family, then the tribe, was the only organized element. From those days arose the villages, the cities, then the nations, and finally empires. As for culture and thought, there has been a religious epoch, a metaphysical epoch, and now, surely, we have reached the epoch of science and technology.

The structure of a civilization may change. From time to time the emphasis may be placed on different values, but one thing always remains immutable: the family, that is to say, the union of man and woman in the sacred bonds of marriage to ensure the survival of the human race. In each epoch this fundamental community has found its own way of developing in harmony with the elements of culture and civilization surrounding it.

The need to found a family, the need of a man to love his wife and to be a father, the need of a woman to love her husband and to be a mother – these needs are stronger for most people than any urge to create works of art or to build a city.

Aristotle, in the wake of Plato, saw in this deep-seated wish for parenthood a participation in divine eternity.

The desire of a man and of a woman to leave behind them an image of themselves is based upon an instinct for immortality. There is in the human being a natural need to give life that is more profound than other needs. Human nature will always urge man and woman to found a home. It will always urge woman to become a loving and gentle mother. But however strong human nature may be, civilization and society can always, in varying degrees, exert an influence upon the human mentality of the day. Civilization can develop without worrying about the family. It will even at times, for technical or economic reasons, act in a way which, instead of helping nature in its sacred function of procreation, may tend to make man forget the nobility of this task and the indispensable conditions which should accompany it. A civilization can so insist upon certain aspects of the human being – upon its liberty for example – that even motherhood may appear not as a glory but as a fetter to woman. It can put so much emphasis upon the harmonious and mysterious aspects of love that the need for faithfulness and constancy is forgotten. It can also so emphasize economic values and the necessity for human success in external things that man's capacity for emotion and so for all true friendship is weakened.

The transition from the religious and metaphysical ages to the age of science has unfortunately been effected so far not by addition but by replacement. In many ways science has been used not to emphasize but to weaken the essential truths of faith and metaphysics. Man is a being of creativeness as well as of faith and love, intelligence and reason. To fulfil himself, these functions must harmonize within his personality. Creativeness, science, technology – without moral reason, without justice, without friendship, above all without religion and loving faith in God – will tend to make of man a heartless automated thing. In its application for man's uses, science should be inspired by human and divine justice, the only guarantee of the integrity of what is inviolate and unique in mankind.

Our transition to the age of technology has not been effected without a certain amount of confusion. The little community so essential to life and to society has suffered some rather trying shocks. The amazing development of economics and material civilization has brought a crisis upon the family. It is time for men with serious responsibilities in society to take stock together of the problems facing us. The future is in our hands. It is up to us to direct the course of our civilization that it may remain really and truly human, that is to say, favourable to all that is essentially human.

The prodigious development of science and technology should teach us that man is not merely destined to know the universe but to transform it so that it can ultimately become an instrument for the unification of all humanity. This modern age is also one of huge industrial and commercial cities which exercise an irresistible attraction upon the mass of people, upon the multitude of those engaged in manual tasks. The modern city, with all its administrative complexities and economic demands, gives rise necessarily to a new crisis in our culture – in humanism and, more particularly, in the family and in religion.

My wife and I have often spoken of our fears and hopes in this regard. We have talked of our fears because we have been impressed by the tendency to forget that the union of man with woman carries noble and great responsibilities that are fundamentally sacred, and that the raising of children depends upon the devotion of their parents. We have not been without hope, however, because we are confident that Canadians in facing up to the problems that exist will be able to work together in building a society that is more aware of truly human values, and so, more respectful of family ties.

From this hope came the idea of the conference. Friends whom we approached responded beyond our fondest expectations. They heard our appeal. They have worked hard and long. The fruits of their labours are manifest today. To them, to all who – like you – have given of their time and resources so that this conference might take place, my wife and I express our heartfelt thanks.

This idea has germinated and blossomed through the visible aid of Divine Providence and through the untiring efforts of you and of others who have made themselves the instruments of God.

I need hardly tell you the importance of your task. Amongst you are experts who specialize in every field concerning the family. Many of you are doing what you might call "field work." Others are specialists in the ways of learning and theory. Together you will survey the present state of the Canadian family. You will investigate honestly and realistically those factors which, in our society, tend to be either a danger to the family or a strength.

It is for us to prepare the future, not a future which would be a poor copy of the past but a new one fit for new requirements. We can do it. Without bemoaning the past, we can and we must direct our efforts in such a way that the family will continue in the future to hold its unique place in society with its human values and ideals. It is for us to prepare for our children and grandchildren a civilization more propitious to the spiritual development of man.

Seeing you gathered here today I have the impression that one of the objectives of the conference has already been reached. For months past men and women of a variety of creeds and cultures have been working efficiently together. It is a wonderful example of unity, a great hope for the future.

Many of the observations I make to you today are those of a man who has had the experience of living in a number of countries, of conversing with many people, and above all has had the joy of living happily with the wife and children that the Lord has given to him. It is not as a philosopher but as the father of a family that I speak to you.

There is an ancient tradition recorded about a thousand years before our era, and undoubtedly told by generation to generation since the earliest times of remotest antiquity. It tells of woman as the sole friend of man as his his equal: his own bones, his own flesh and blood. According to it, Eve is the wife and companion. She is the equal of man and his friend. And these two persons, in their love and their unity, are the image of God.

This first and oldest view changed over the ages so that womankind was frequently considered as inferior to man. Even Aristotle, one of the greatest thinkers ever to concern himself with human relations, could not conceive of a perfect friendship between men and women; there were too many inequalities between them. The role of women in society was reduced to nothing more than maternity. Man, on the other hand, could by his speculative intelligence delve into divine things. But in Israel during Aristotle's time maternity played a more important role because of the association of race with faith in God. From the Jewish people, from a Jewish woman, Christ was born.

The Jewish people felt what Aristotle did not: that the woman is not only the mother of children but the unique friend and confidante of man. This view was first recorded by Plutarch and St. Paul.

The ancients used to say that a friend is one's other self. Two friends are one soul in two bodies. This need to love and to be loved is profoundly real. In friendship new strength is given and a new sense of security received. But, for friendship to be true, it should be based on a promise. The impetus of love must be established and stabilized in what one might call a deep and irrevocable decision of fidelity.

The need to procreate is related to love and friendship, founded upon a promise. It is a natural mystery. The conception of the child and so the existence of future generations is in effect associated – or should be associated – with true friendship and love, that is with the union of two human beings who, transcending egoism, seek only each other's good. In creating the universe in love God intended that the very existence of human beings should find its purpose in love. From the highest relationship between human beings on earth, from that which permits us most to resemble the Almighty, namely, love and friendship, comes the very existence of future generations. Thus we see the richness of human love. It is not introverted. It is above all not a desire to take. It is not merely happiness between two people. It is fecundity. Through children, the manifestations and fruits of such a union, it is the giving of one's self to the universe and to humanity, and particularly to God, the author of life and creation. Conjugal love manifests itself in children who are part of man and woman. So far as the world is concerned, the children are their work, testimony of their reciprocal devotion and love.

One should ask whether the family does in fact always play the fundamental role for which it has been equipped by nature and the grace of God in the early education of children. Are parents always conscious of their duties and as thoughtful as they might be of their infants? Through negligence, or lack of effort, and sometimes even under some special pretext of health, do they not sometimes sacrifice the moral welfare of the child to their own comfort or to his purely physical well-being? Has not psycho-analysis emphasized more than ever before than the little child needs above all to be loved, that is to say, to find serene, understanding, and generous people who allow themselves to be loved and to love?

The question is whether present living and working conditions and above all the mental outlook of parents are favourable or harmful to their first essential duty as parents?

Even the smallest, simplest flower needs cultivation. The soil must be nourishing. Water and an appropriate temperature are required. What is true in the vegetable and animal kingdoms is even more true in the human kingdom. Just as it took humanity thousands of years to acquire culture, so every human being grows slowly. This growth is not merely an infallible and instinctive upsurge of life, some sort of will-power that draws its strength from itself. Such a view of nature is not in keeping with biological fact. A flower must be nourished. It is the sun's light which somehow draws out the flowers. Certainly there is an instinctive growth, but there is also this call or attraction of light, as also there is the rainfall which provides the seed with necessary nourishment and enables it to grow.

To be well balanced, most human beings need a loving mother who helps in the development of deep affections, and a judicious and kindly father who helps in the acquisition of self-discipline. A child needs to imitate both the mother's devotion and unselfishness and the father's prudence and wisdom.

I know that psychologists agree that for a child really to have the qualities of truth, goodness, and generosity, for him to be unselfish, for him to put justice and truth above comfort, pleasure, or ambition, the parents by their example must inspire imitation. The child imitates that which he loves. The above virtues develop through the close and habitual contact between parents and children. Today, as in times gone by and perhaps the more so because of the gravity of our situation, our country needs citizens prepared to sacrifice their personal interest.

Canada has a prodigious heritage. Ours is a unique situation not only historically but geographically also. We are not a powerful country. We cannot be one of the great military powers. But we can and must find our true vocation in the best sense, as a country opposed to pure materialism.

But to achieve this we must reconquer and resume our spiritual heritage. Man is not merely made of flesh and bone. He is not merely a collection of atoms and molecules. He has a heart. He has a spirit. Our country is the offspring of Western civilization which itself is rooted in the theistic humanism of the Greeks and Romans, in the religious faith of Israel, in the faith of Isaac and Jacob, in the God of Abraham.

Let us find once more the flame that lit the way for the first missionaries and pioneers. Let us again find that flame which at times has so often been hidden under a bushel, experience it, and communicate it. It is humanity's hope.

To my way of thinking, the best and surest way of developing generous and idealistic hearts, of giving the community men and women who are well balanced and conscious of their responsibilities to their country, is to protect the family, for the family – far from opposing the interests of society – is capable of giving to the universe the human beings who are prepared to put justice and truth before their own personal interests.

At opening ceremony, Canadian Conference on the Family, 7 June 1964

DURING THE PAST FORTY YEARS, AS WE MOVED ABOUT VARIOUS PARTS OF this and other countries of the Atlantic community, both my wife and I have been impressed frequently and forcefully by the vital importance of family life. Meeting and talking with people of all conditions, we have witnessed the inner strength and confidence of those nurtured in the love of a true family, and we have observed the lonely hopelessness and moral difficulty of those deprived of the support that only a family can provide. Bearing this in mind, we were anxious to see established in our native land an enduring association of many professions dedicated to the reinforcement of family living.

In furtherance of this purpose, we invited prominent sociologists, social workers, scholars, and religious leaders of several denominations to come together on June 7, 1964, in a Conference on the Family. The response to our appeal was a moving testimony to the concern felt by so many important and influential leaders in our society ...

... To our delight, their acceptance of the challenge was immediate, and bore fruit in the creation of the organization which its founders very generously named "The Vanier Institute of the Family." Our joy at this deeply gratifying result was crowned with the agreement of Dr. Penfield to accept the position of President.

The founders and initial directors of the newly created institute were citizens of admirable distinction iñ various walks of the country's life. They selected a hundred active members from all the provinces. This ensures the involvement and participation of every element in Canadian society.

The Institute of the Family has adopted, as its ideal, the happiness and integrity of the Canadian family. The intention is not to advocate a return to the past but to explore ways to strengthen and reinforce family life in a contemporary world. We are convinced that the quality of this country's family life will determine the character of the entire nation. The means by which the Institute hopes to contribute to a better understanding and a promotion of family unity and happiness are the following:

First, in the field of research and liaison, the co-ordination of work at present underway or already accomplished on the nature of the family, and of the family's reactions to the new conditions of our present age;

Second, the organization of conferences and seminars, both national and regional in scope;

Third, in the field of education, the propagation as extensively as possible of the discoveries made concerning family life and the role of the family in the formation of personality and civic responsibility. This dissemination of information would have, as its goal, the betterment of family and society alike.

The Institute is not, of course, a welfare organization and will not attempt to duplicate the excellent work already being done by organizations in the social welfare field.

Four major projects have already been approved by the Institute's Board of Directors:

First, a large-scale survey of Canadian family attitudes and requirements;

Second, a study of family education available not only in schools, but also from churches, community and government agencies, labour unions and other institutions;

Third, the establishment of a central library which will provide a national reference centre for documentation on the family; and

Fourth, a study of specific types of families and of their place in a specific social context, such as families of ethnic minorities, rural families, slum dwellers, and families whose parents have separated.

The task before the Institute, and indeed before all those who share our concern for the welfare of the family and the future of our society, is an enormous and urgent one. It will require dedication and devotion to a noble cause, and the erudition and understanding of a great scholar, ... Dr. Penfield.

From Foreword to Man and His Family, *a collection of lectures by Dr. Wilder Penfield, the Governor-General's last published writing, completed just two days before his death*

WHAT A TREMENDOUS HOPE FOR THE FUTURE OF OUR COUNTRY LIES IN OUR children, provided only that our families remain united and strong, and provided we give these eager enquiring minds the guidance and leadership they deserve. I say provided our families remain united and strong, for surely the family unit is the core and essence of any nation, and the surest indication of the future strength and integrity of that nation.

The role of the family is not limited to ensuring the mere physical preservation of the species. The family is the cradle of moral and spiritual values as well, values that are every bit as essential to our survival as a civilized people. Parents who are united in ties of affection and self-giving, and who are aware of the importance of intelligent counsel and example, are the first to open the hearts and minds of children to the values of the spirit, values of truth, justice, and religion. The parents plant the first seeds of love, generosity, and selflessness, and thus fashion and guide youth on the way to becoming citizens devoted to noble causes for the common good.

At a dinner given by the Premier of Saskatchewan, Regina, 17 June 1965

WE KNOW THAT THE QUALITIES WE TEACH OUR CHILDREN WILL DOMINATE their characters and personalities for the rest of their lives. Building character is something we cannot leave for adult life because by then, to a large extent, the mould is set. The nature and greatness of our society and our country tomorrow are being determined now by the training we give and the example we set our children.

I am sorry to say that there are many cases of parents who, preoccupied with their problems, distracted by the television or other methods of self-indulgence, never consider their full responsibilities towards their children, and treat them with indifference, or worse – as a necessary nuisance. Their questions are ignored and their efforts to improve their knowledge are given no help, much less encouragement. They learn only that wanting to learn is an irritation to others and before they even enter school their outgoing tendencies have been sealed within a shell of self-defence and withdrawal. Strange that the children's parents are then unable to understand the failure of their offspring to make better grades in school or even to show an interest in their studies! The children's first failures are met, not with love and understanding, but with further recriminations and once again the mould is set. The rejected child becomes the drop-out; the drop-out, the delinquent; the delinquent, the despairing and despondent adult unable to take his place in society, much less contribute to the well-being of his fellows and his country.

Sometimes our children's development poses delicate and difficult problems, both for our patience and for our understanding. Such occasions should be ones of challenge but not of despair. Two basic ingredients will provide a foundation for our relationships which will weather any storm and create within our children the basis for characters that will stand them through life. These two qualities are simply love and respect: a love for the child that seeks nothing but the child's welfare; a respect for the child that helps us to regard him, not as a mere possession, but as a creation of God entrusted to our care.

We must not imagine, however, that these qualities will develop within ourselves automatically. They need careful nurturing and intelligent attention. The art of parenthood is not one for the amateur or for one who relies entirely on intuition. Parenthood is a profession which requires as much intelligent training and study as many others and is, indeed, much more noble.

Certainly love and respect, if they are to be developed to their utmost, must be given rationally and consciously as well as intuitively. We cannot hope to develop them fully without an awareness of the spiritual values they imply. These values we must nurture and encourage within ourselves if we are to convey them to our children, and convey them we must, if even our simplest hopes for their inner well-being are to be satisfied.

At a public meeting on Family Life, Sydney, 25 May 1966

WE HAVE HAD A FEW AMUSING EXPERIENCES DURING OUR TRAVELS THROUGH Canada. You may like this one perhaps. One little girl, after I had proclaimed a holiday in the name of the Queen, was most enthusiastic. I heard from her mother later that she had said: "You know, I like our Governor-General. He is a very nice man, he gives us holidays. I hope he lives a long time, because I am going to begin saving up money. I like him so much that I want to save up enough to attend his funeral when he dies." That is the best tribute I have ever had.

At a dinner for the Judges of the County and District Courts of Ontario,
Toronto, 9 April 1965

General Vanier on occasion received letters from school-children asking for
sample autographs. He found some of these quite amusing:

Dear Sir, I am starting a collection of different people and would like you to be one ...
Dear Sir, I would like your autograph and some from any members of your family who can write ...

WE ARE NOT PRESENTED WITH AN IMPOSSIBLE IMPASSE IN OUR HOPES FOR the future of the family. Quite the contrary, we have gained an insight into those avenues which we may best pursue to regain the strength and unity that the family knew in times past. Most parents continue conscientiously to seek the maximum welfare of their families, but cannot help being disturbed by our initial findings, based as these findings are on statistics for juvenile delinquency and social disintegration. Perhaps it is now the time to strengthen the confidence of those who, with the best of wills, are still anxious and perplexed.

We need, I believe, fully to understand the nature of the changes now affecting the family. The greatest of these, it goes without saying, is the decline in the structure of authority within the family and, for that matter, within the community at large. In previous periods of our history this authority had never – or at best only very rarely – been challenged or even come into serious question. In our present society, however, a strong paternal authority is no longer in vogue and discipline within the family is much less clear or well defined. The chief result of this decline has been new uncertainty and moral confusion in our young people. It seems to many people as if society has lost control of many of its young people and that their behaviour has reached the point of being not only unacceptable to the community but against even their own interests.

I do not suggest that this position is the result solely of a decline in the structure of authority within the family. Many factors have played a role; not the least of these has been the change in the position of the importance of religion in the life of the family and in society itself. Religion has become much less of a family affair in which family prayers, grace at meals and regular attendance as a family at church or synagogue were a part of family life. It is an overworked axiom, but it is true, "a family that prays together stays together," not so much because common prayer is just another group activity but rather because religion is something profound and basic which draws on the well-springs of family unity. A picnic or a party can also be an exercise in unity but the unity engendered may be little more than surface friendship. Prayer, by contrast, goes to the very essence of our being, touches all that we feel important in life. The bonds of fellowship which the sharing of prayer creates are links which even the strongest forces of adversity cannot break.

In many ways, the place given to religion has diminished in the family. Religion itself has suffered from the onslaught of new philosophies from outside and new sophistication from within. The stories and parables which, in the old days, provided so clear and uncomplicated guidance have now been rationalized and diluted beyond recognition. The new morality may be more palatable to the subtle reasoning of adult intelligence, but it no longer provides the simple statement of faith which parents could pass for the guidance of their children. For that matter, our present sophistication in religion has confused many adults; how much more so must it puzzle and bewilder our young people. If parents themselves do not understand the tenets of their faith in crystal clarity, they will be too reticent or even too embarrassed to try to pass these tenets to their young. The tragic result is that even an older person, fully convinced of his religion, may yet be hesitant or even quite unable to convey his faith to his children. Often the heaven-sent idealism of youth withers away for lack of clear direction. A boy gathers materials for a temple but when he reaches manhood, he settles for a woodshed.

The changing position of women in the family is another factor which has led to brand-new social patterns. The greater degree of independence granted to women and the new possibilities for married women to continue in their work or profession have set new standards by which old loyalties have suffered. No longer is a home given the dominant importance that once it held.

Changes in the working patterns of the men of the families have also played their part. The increase in shift work unsettles old living habits and sometimes makes the sharing of family life impossible. Some occupations take men away from home altogether for considerable periods of time and the increase in "moonlighting" – the holding of a second occupation – has a similar effect. The centrifugal forces acting on the family are sometimes so many and so strong that the home becomes less a home than a boarding house; the family less a family than a circle of strangers who meet only intermittently.

These and other developments have led in turn to the decline in what the sociologists call the kinship group, the concentration of three generations under one roof which, in previous times, did much to enhance the understanding and education of the younger members of the family. The grandparents reinforced the pattern of authority within the family while, at the same time, broadening the grandchildren's acquaintanceship with the adult world.

Changing patterns of work and living standards seem to have created new emphasis on material aspirations for the family. The growth of our cities has led to new mobility in our society and to a greater tendency for young people to live apart from their family and seek their independence early in life. The increasing influence of the mass media must not be overlooked and the greater power that advertising holds over the thought patterns of our society.

Finally, there has been a new awareness and a new emphasis on the importance of the child's personality. It has been well said that, whereas in the nineteenth century children were taught that they owed everything to their parents, in this, the middle of the twentieth century, parents are taught that they owe everything to their children.

This new importance assumed by the younger generation has had several consequences, some of them good, some of them somewhat less so. On the one side there has developed a new concern for the underprivileged child, for the abandoned or the orphan. This concern has been paralleled with greater attention to all persons in need: the indigent, the handicapped, and the elderly. On the other hand, the new importance given to our youth has also led to a widening of the gap between the generations. For all that, the cries of dismay heard so frequently from the older generation, dismay with the rebellious non-conformism of adolescence, may well reflect a mistaken interpretation of what is really happening. We have always had our rebels and eccentrics and we must keep our sence of proportion. The reassuring fact of which we must not lose sight is that most Canadian families still maintain through all the vicissitudes of change a basic solidarity and a moral cohesion seen in happy and peaceful unity. Parents still enjoy the companionship of their children in spite of the disappearance of the old patriarchal authority.

What can we learn from those many families who seem to have retained their essential unity and integrity throughout the many changes in our present-day society? What are the keys to their success, that we may emphasize and further develop them? Might it not be that the first of these is the retention of those old and tried virtues of frankness and honesty in family relationships? In the greater sophistication of current society these virtues may have changed their names or appear in different forms but they still are the best and firmest bridge between the generations and thus still foster the understanding, the respect, and the strength of character necessary for personal development.

There is a saying in French that the more things change the more they remain basically the same. The fruits of the spirit have not changed a particle since St. Paul first enumerated them nineteen centuries ago. Love, patience, understanding, unselfishness, mutual respect, and a sense of service – these are qualities which may find new channels for their employment but whose nature remains forever the same. Our duty as parents surely becomes simply the interpretation of these values.

But, if our duty is clear, its fulfilment is not so simple. Family relationships have become, in this modern age, a science much more subtle and complicated than ever existed in times past. To begin with, the refinements of psychology have made clear the subtle ramifications of human behaviour, the hidden motivations, the facades and the paradoxes of modern mentalities; secondly, the number of new and distracting influences on family life, the greater diversity of attractions vying for the attention of our young, the new importance of their acceptance by their peers, the new standards imposed by advertising and the mass media, the many bewilderments thrust upon our young by technical advances – these are profound and far-reaching influences on the structure of our families and to understand them and to make allowance for them is no longer a task which can be left to sentiment and intuition. There is, in short, no place for the amateur when it comes to bringing up the child of the twentieth century. We must all be professionals of a sort – by which I mean that we must study and understand the complex forces that affect our society and our children's psychologies.

We who would defend family values must stand up and be counted. Modern civilization seems to have the curious conviction that it can get by without the existence of strong family bonds. Much of our technical progress and social emancipation seem almost at odds with the old virtues of the pioneer family. The tyranny of materialism may even force its unthinking victims to place "keeping up with the Joneses" before the sacred duties of even beginning the formation of a family. Our modern democratic stress on the independence of the individual is all too easily mistaken for a call to self-indulgence, to such an extent, indeed, that simpler souls may be induced to sacrifice the infinite joys of motherhood for the pale and passing pleasures of personal liberty. The foes, in short, whether by purpose or default, that are ranged in opposition to family values are numerous and potent. If we are to combat them, we must make clear our position and be sure of our arsenal. Above all, we must see clearly the virtues which have established our families and our nation in the past.

We must be flexible and adaptable in our guidance of our children but we must also be confident of ourselves and sure of the worth of these virtues. There is no room for doubt in the guidance and example we show our young.

At the First Annual Meeting Dinner of the Vanier Institute of the Family, Government House, 27 October 1966

Youth

YOU KNOW HOW DELIGHTED MY WIFE AND I ARE TO MEET THE CHILDREN OF our land. The reason is simple: we see in them what our country will become in the years before us. I wonder how many of us realize the importance of this fact – the importance of devoting the time and effort necessary to ensure that our children are being given the finest possible education both in mind and spirit. Tell me the character of a nation's young people and I will tell you the future of the nation. Tell me what occupies the minds of a country's young men, whether their thoughts be selfish or noble, self-indulgent or disciplined, self-centred or dedicated; tell me this and I will describe for you the future of that nation in the world.

A country's greatest potential asset is its young people. Youth is the opportunity to learn what is really valuable in life to become really worth while. It is up to us of the older generations to make sure these opportunities do not go unheeded, to make sure that nothing stands in the way of their fulfilment.

Young people rely on emotion rather than on experience – let us whose spirits are a little jaded thank God that they do. Enthusiasm without experience must be guided, but experience without spirit is cold and ineffective.

We can learn from our young people as well as teach them. So long as we are close to them, we too will remain young in heart and mind; so long as we devote our maximum efforts to their upbringing, we can rest assured that the future of our country will be in good hands.

Reply to address of welcome of the Mayor of Deep River, Ontario,
7 October 1966

Shortly after completing a tour throughout western Canada, General Vanier recounted his impressions during a radio and television Message broadcast on 1 July 1965:

WE MET AND SPOKE TO MANY THOUSANDS OF CHILDREN. WE WERE MUCH impressed by their appearance. They were enthusiastic, healthy, and intelligent. No one can doubt that the future of Canada has great promise when it will be in the hands of such bright and eager young people, providing only that they are given the leadership and guidance they need and deserve.

I THINK I AM TELLING YOU NO SECRET WHEN I SAY THAT SOME OF THE happiest moments of my wife's and my own sojourn at Government House have been spent with the young men of the Ottawa Boys' Club here and at Rideau Hall. Some of my more solemn friends cannot explain how I manage to feel like a young boy myself sometimes. They tell me it is not fair for a man so old to behave as if he were very young. They ask how I can avoid being as solemn as they at such a solemn age. I tell them the answer is very simple: they have only to take a large infusion of the Boys' Club once or twice a year and they will catch, as quickly as they catch the measles, a handsome case of cheerfulness, good fun, and high spirits.

Young people have wonderful qualities, qualities which all of us can imitate and encourage to our own advantage. Their very zest for life is like an explosion, like a rocket, if you like – but a rocket going off in all directions does no one any good and inevitably ends up by doing everyone a lot of harm. A rocket must be carefuly guided if it is to render service and accomplishment. ... guided missiles are important and guided boys are even more so. Give these young minds a target for their enthusiasm, wholesomeness of mind and body, willingness to work for one another, discipline to bring out their best instincts, respect for hard work, and dedication. These are the objectives we must set before our young people if they themselves are to realize their full potential and if our country is to achieve the greatness destiny has offered it.

Unveiling a portrait of the late Fred McCann, at the Ottawa Boys' Club, 23 February 1966

THE AFFLUENCE OF OUR SOCIETY ... GIVES US A SORT OF SMUG SELF-satisfaction which finds its expression sometimes in another word: apathy. Need I remind you of what happens when apathy in public affairs becomes widespread: community leadership falls into the hands of the demagogue and the fortune-seeker. The history of man tells the tale of great empires which fell, not from outward assault but from inward decay and moral degeneration.

If we are to combat this drift towards apathy we must begin with our youth. More than half of all Canadians today are younger than twenty-two. The need for firm guidance and inspired teaching by their elders is now perhaps more essential than it has ever been, not only for youth's own well-being but for the very future of our country.

We live in an age of moral uncertainty. Many traditional social beliefs have been challenged and cast into doubt. The result has been a temptation among parents to abdicate responsibility in the formation of their children's minds.

The youth of our country appear to be dissatisfied with us, their parents. I don't blame them. I am not very proud of what we have done – or perhaps left undone.

Are we giving them the guidance they require, the inspiration they should have if they are to attain fulfilment? Are we giving them a cause to which they can dedicate their efforts, a cause which will bring out all that is noble within them? Or could it be that we are obsessed with goals that are far from noble, with material causes which offer nothing but emptiness to the spirit? How often in the emptiness of our society do the brave young shoots of nobility and compassion wither and die on the barren ground of material values!

Message to the Nation, New Year 1966

During an address given at the Spring Convocation at McGill University, Montreal, on 30 May 1960, General Vanier made reference to certain excesses which had become evident among the younger generation, but he hastened to add the following remarks:

I SHOULD BE THE FIRST TO ADMIT THAT ALL THE FAULTS ARE NOT ON THE side of the young. At a recent conference on Youth held in Washington, a speaker declared that "the basic problem of the young ... is the apathy, perfidy and poor example of the adult generations." The conference concluded: "Before we can expect more from our youth, we must demand more from ourselves. The family must be strengthened, the home restored to the honoured place it once held, parents must honour their ideals through daily use."

Personally I believe that many of today's currents of anger are sparked by the materialism present in our society. We are told that man shall not live by bread alone. Perhaps some of the present rebels are searching through the mists and fogs for the dignity of man. Yet, as they are lacking in personal standards and in self-respect, they come to dislike themselves and are driven to find relief in anger. Speaking for the older generations, I think I can say that we are not at all happy with the sort of world we have produced. Our material progress may have been great, but what of the spiritual? Mere numbers tend to impress us, while we forget that any given organization has its ideal size ...

... To the angry young men and even to you normal, well-adjusted graduates, I say: If you want a better world you must work for it. Let your anger be positive and constructive. Run for Parliament, take an interest in the affairs of your city or province, even if it means taking time off from your business or career.

Governor-General Vanier delivering his New Year's Message to the nation, 1960

The Governor-General receives an enthusiastic welcome from some of his younger constituents at Churchill in 1961

The Governor-General and his two immediate predecessors, Vincent Massey (left) and Earl Alexander of Tunis, at the Montreal Men's Press Club in 1961

With winners in the Dominion Drama Festival in Montreal 1961. At left, John Holmes, director of Toronto's Drao Players, and the company's Michael Zenon. At right, Phyllis Whissell of St. Catharines, Ontario, Community Players

The Governor-General visits Agnes Hardisty in
Fort Simpson, N.W.T., during a northern tour in 1961

At Camp Valcartier in March 1964

The Governor-General and Madame Vanier viewing construction at the site of
Expo 1967 in May 1965, with Robert F. Shaw, deputy commissioner-general of
the exposition

With boy scouts Roderick (left) and Reginald Groome
of Montreal in 1964

His Excellency during an inspection of the dockyard facilities at the Mackenzie
River port of Bell Rock, N.W.T., in 1961. At right, Inspector Carl Doey, honorary
aide de camp

On receiving an honorary degree from the University of Toronto, February 1960

The gun carriage bearing the coffin of Governor-General Vanier past the National War Memorial in Ottawa, 8 March 1967

Give a thought to the youth that will come after you. Help them to find their roots, show them that there are answers to life's problems, however hard. I look to you to teach the children of today that self-sacrifice can be more rewarding than self-indulgence. If you can do all or any of these things you will become like to Prometheus, stealing from heaven the sacred fire to make it available to your fellow-men.

On various occasions General Vanier stressed the qualities which he felt should motivate the young people of today:

A YOUNG MIND SHOULD BE DEVOID OF ANY OF THE SHALLOW PREJUDICES which unfortunately are all too contagious in an older generation. You should be willing and anxious to learn anything that is good. You should be able to distinguish what is generous and loving from that which is selfish and petty. You should seek always to search for new horizons and accept new challenges. Only as you learn more will you realize how little you really know.

This brings me to a quality one likes to associate with youth: the ability, once dedicated to a cause, to appreciate discipline and self-denial. Don't imagine that this quality can be retained throughout life without a conscious and sometimes agonizing effort. Sometimes I think that life in Canada has become easy. Things are just a little too comfortable. It takes a strong will to resist the temptation to slip into a rut of laziness and self-satisfaction and mediocrity. If you are to accomplish anything in your life, you must learn at the earliest possible age that nothing worth while can be accomplished without some sacrifice, that no man can lead others until he has first learned to lead and discipline himself.

At the inspection of the Ashbury Cadet Corps, Ottawa, 8 May 1965

PERMIT ME TO SAY FRANKLY AND SIMPLY THAT OUR YOUNG PEOPLE TODAY need discipline, discipline of body, of heart, and of spirit. Discipline is the basis without which the character of the child, and subsequently of the man, cannot be properly formed.

Does the word "discipline" alarm you? Don't let it. It is too beautiful a word to deprive it of its true meaning, that of "disciple." Each one of us should be both a master and a disciple at the same time, a master by our example, a disciple by our obedience to natural and divine law.

At a banquet on the occasion of the Twenty-Fifth Anniversary of the Federation of Catholic Scouts of the Province of Quebec, 24 February 1960 (translation)

COURAGE IS A QUALITY WHICH MUST BE CAREFULLY NURTURED. COURAGE is built on a foundation of conviction and dedication as well as on sound training and knowledge.

Youth is the time of life when seeds of training and of guidance fall on the most fruitful ground. Every period of life has its special opportunities and its peculiar dangers, but youth is the time when greatness can most easily be grafted, as well as being the time when temptations can be most damaging. It is during our younger days that our spirit is most open and anxious to learn. It is the spring season in our development as men and it is during this season, more than any other, that character assumes the form and nature which will carry it through life.

No man but a fool would claim to be the master of his destiny but every man, with God's help, can be the architect of his own character. Character alone determines whether life is even worth the living; it follows, therefore, that as the character of our young people goes, so will the stature of our nation.

At a Boy Scout Investiture at Government House, 25 October 1966

In view of his keen interest in young people, it is not surprising that General Vanier frequently stressed the importance of organizations for youth:

I COMMEND ... TO YOUR ATTENTION THE PROFOUND AND ENDURING VALUE which your children can gain from participation in any of several organizations devoted to the training of youth ...

Certainly a young person today who does not belong to at least one such group is missing half the fun and half the education he or she needs and deserves. Fun – because the wholesome friendships, the working together, and the common pride in joint achievements add new dimensions to anyone's enjoyment of life; education – because a realization of the value of self-discipline, hard work, mutual respect, and dedication to a worthy cause is something which adds stature, and maturity, and wisdom which will enrich one's entire life.

We are not born with these qualities, at least in a developed sense; we have to be shown them by example, we have to learn them, and it is a sacred duty as parents for us to make sure that they are given attention. We must never abdicate our responsibilities, for the basic qualities of honour, duty, and responsibility, and the virtues of love, unselfishness, and dedication are neither casual nor uncertain: they are the only realities in life, and they are eternal.

At a dinner given by the Premier of Saskatchewan, Regina, 17 June 1965

SERVICE AND COURAGE LIE AT THE HEART OF SCOUTING. WHEN THESE qualities are manifested by one or other of its members, the movement is strengthened. In turn, scouting reinforces the national character. Canada's most valuable national asset is youth – and scouting has a most important part to play in its training and formation. Scouting gets the full value out of youth by training it without blunting the edge of its spirit.

In the first place it gives discipline, without which no human being can be quite happy. Man's natural lot is to serve, and, at its best, his is a free service in which he accepts of his own free will the obligation of living in the human community.

In the second place, scouting gives companionship and develops new interests in life. The true genius and inspiration of the movement is that it weds the aspirations and fancies of youth to the wider issues of life.

Thirdly, scouting gives youngsters a code of conduct, something to live up to. In these days of unrest and uncertainty it is of the highest value that youth have something firm to hold to, some honourable standard to live by.

At a Boy Scout Investiture, 3 November 1964

EACH OF YOU MAY TAKE PROFOUND PRIDE AND SATISFACTION IN THIS occasion. I need hardly tell you that it is one which brings a sense of deep and abiding joy to me. I congratulate you who have been instrumental in bringing to fruition this great achievement.

The signing of this agreement between the Boy Scouts of Canada and les Scouts catholiques du Canada, Secteur français, is not a mere functional act of affiliation between the two groups, it is much more than that. This agreement is a ringing declaration of faith and hope and brotherhood: faith in the basic ability of men of goodwill to work together in harmony and mutual respect; hope that others may be inspired to make equally dramatic steps towards a true unity of our country, the unity not of a neighborhood of strangers, but a brotherhood of friends. This agreement is a declaration for all Canadians that whatsoever is worth while can and must be done in unity. No other lesson for our country in our centennial year could be more important or imperative.

That this lesson should be given by the scouting movement in Canada can only add to its vitality and inspiration. Youth is the time when a nation's future is decided. The character we instil in our young people today will decide the destiny of our nation tomorrow. If we invest in faith and hope and brotherhood, we can be more than positive that Canada will reap dividends for a century to come.

We of older generations, who are proud of our country, therefore owe it to Canada to guide our youth along the paths of unselfishness and mutual affection. Let us never imagine that such service to our young people is any sort of a sacrifice, for in reality it is also service to ourselves. If ever we find that we are falling out of sympathy with our young people, then I think that our work on earth is just about over. Whatever our physical age may be, we have grown old in heart and spirit. People do not really age by merely living a number of years. I am convinced that we grow old only by deserting our ideals. We are, in fact, as old as our doubts and our despair, but we are as young as our faith and our hope, especially faith and hope in our youth, which is, after all, the same as saying our faith and our hope in our country's future.

§ I am bold enough to say that this date will be remembered as a memorable one in Canadian history. The French-speaking division of les Scouts catholiques, and the Boy Scouts of Canada, through their affiliation, will be able to play a role of primary importance in promoting the unity of our country.

As you know, and as I have repeated many times since my nomination as governor-general, the three great concerns that have occupied so much of my thoughts and hopes are youth, national unity, and spiritual values. In scouting I find the expression of all three of them at the same time.

I congratulate all those concerned with the scouting movement and particularly those who provide its leadership. Your work is admirable, not only in the field of human relations, but also in the realm of moral and spiritual considerations. Leading our young people along the paths of discipline, personal initiative, mutual assistance, and service to one's neighbour in response to God's love: here surely is an undertaking of transcendant nobility. Here, surely, is the real flame of life, which breathes warmth and light into the relations of man with man, which unifies these relations and makes of them something divine.§

At the ceremony marking the signing of an agreement to affiliate the Boy Scouts of Canada and les Scouts catholiques du Canada, Secteur français, held at Government House, 22 February 1967

§Translated from the French.

Man and His Intellect

Education and Its Purpose

UNIVERSAL EDUCATION IS TODAY THE NECESSARY COUNTERPART OF UNIVER-sal suffrage. It is the essential preparation for those who are about to find their place in our complex industrial society.

On laying the foundation-stone of Woodroffe High School, Ottawa,
21 June 1960

NOW, AS NEVER BEFORE, CANADA'S PROGRESS, WEALTH, AND SECURITY DE-pend on the educational level, technical knowledge, and skill of her people. The important man today is the highly trained worker because modern technology is reducing, and often cutting out completely the old forms of hand labour. As a striking example of this, 400,000 men have stopped work-ing on farms over the last ten years while agricultural output has remained at a record level.

It is safe to say that these changes will affect the majority of Canadian families. At the moment seventy per cent of employment is to a large extent closed to young people who leave school before graduating. Yet I am told that two-thirds of all the pupils entering grade one generally fail to obtain a graduation diploma. This is the problem – and it will become still more serious as industry relies more and more on educated and therefore trainable workers to carry out its complex operations.

It seems inevitable that those who leave school before graduation will miss most of the opportunities available in our country; they will cut themselves off from the possibility of training in industry. If they can find work it will probably be employment with little future. They may thus have to face a lifetime of insecurity, accompanied by limited earning power and the prospect of long periods of unemployment.

I see a challenge to all Canadians in this situation. To adults, and more particularly to you who are parents, it means that you must take a greater interest in young people, helping them overcome their problems, and giving them an early and lasting appreciation of the value of education, training, and good citizenship. To you, young people of Canada, it means that not only must you remain in school longer but more of you must seek out apprenticeships, the trade or vocational school, and the technical institute.

To you, Canadian employers, it means that training schemes must be greatly expanded. To you who are already working, it will often mean improving your skills or retraining to prepare for changing times. And to you who are organizing formal education and training, it means a constant search for improvement.

Proclamation for "Commonwealth Technical Training Week in Canada,"
29 May to 4 June 1961

EDUCATION IS PARTLY FACTS AND FIGURES BUT IT IS ALSO THE ACQUIRING of a generous spirit, an open mind, and qualities such as honesty, compassion, and dedication. Make the most of your time in school and you will have no trouble making the most of your adult lives and contributing the most to your country in the century to come.

Message to the pupils of Greendale School, Niagara Falls, written
for publication in June 1967

WHAT ... MAY WE EXPECT FROM FORMAL EDUCATION? IT IS SURELY NOT TOO much to ask that by the time pupils leave school they must not only have acquired certain knowledge but should also be able to communicate effectively. By this I mean that they should be able to convey their ideas both orally and on paper clearly and concisely. Unfortunately it seems that there are many students who are limited in the range of their own ideas. What is more, all too often they are quite unreceptive to any new and perhaps unwelcome thoughts that may be offered them by the outside world. How can we account for this? I think it may be in part because many children spend years studying without ever learning how to communicate properly. They never learn to speak really well, they never learn to listen with discrimination, they never learn to express themselves in writing with clarity and emphasis. Above all, in their schooling they don't get hold of ideas which they would feel a real urge to express. The first need is then for thinkers who can explain themselves, thinkers who will not be swept away by suggestion, by images, by hidden persuasions.

It is hardly less important that today's pupils should be well grounded and initiated in the realms of science and mathematics. Unfortunately, there are some whose knowledge of these subjects is limited to space-fiction. I know that children exist who have an inborn dislike for figures and no particular taste for chemistry or physics. To them science should perhaps be presented under its historical aspect with some explanation of its methods, its purposes, and its limitations. At all events, I think it is necessary to ensure that some of the most intelligent students be not abruptly and prematurely cut off from the world of science because they want to concentrate on, say, languages.

There is a third major field which our schools should throw open. They can help to induce the younger generation to enrich their own lives and the lives of others by the practice and appreciation of the creative arts. I feel that a little practice and active participation is worth a lot of passive appreciation, but even the latter alone is much better than nothing. Already we have a problem of making effective use of the leisure which is now available to us. In the years to come this problem may well grow greater. Non-professional music, painting, theatre, and dancing will surely have an increased part to play.

Finally, I should like to consider what is the purpose that lies behind education. In the past boys and girls were nurtured on the Bible and the Classics. If they left school with some knowledge of ethics and some standards of morality, these standards were largely biblical and classical. This is no longer always the case. There may be some who scoff at the old ideal of the Christian and the Gentleman, but what have they put in its place?

The curriculum should be more than just a list of different subjects. The child should be able to learn something of how they fit together and of the way in which they are related to the purpose of life itself. Education must instil values, it must teach its pupils to love goodness and truth.

To sum up, our schools must concern themselves with communication, with science, with creativity and morality. They will only do this effectively if parents and children form the habit of asking intelligent questions. They must not be satisfied with the easy answer, or the merely plausible answer. Upon the quality of their questioning will depend the depth of their understanding. For we do not only operate with our understanding of things, we are changed by what we comprehend.

At a luncheon of Canadian Clubs, Hamilton, 21 November 1960

MERE SCHOOLING, THE LEARNING OF IDEAS BY ROTE, NEEDS ONLY A FEW highly compressed, carefully preserved ideas, and the sledge-hammer of repetition with which to pound them into the students' minds ...

Cramming ... may look all right but it is really all gloss. The best that can be said about it is that it uses God-given intelligence as a temporary storehouse for facts and figures. Obviously, this is not what intelligence is for. Not long ago, I read that the word "intelligence" is derived from two Latin words *inter* and *legere, inter* meaning "between" and *legere* meaning "to choose." An intelligent person, therefore, is one who has learned "to choose between." The purpose of education in a way can be described as the development of the individual's capacity to make the best choice.

On opening Brock University, St. Catharines, 19 October 1964

TO A LARGE EXTENT, LEARNING, IT SEEMS TO ME, CONSISTS OF REALIZING something to be true that one has been told all along was true. There is a lesson here, I think, for both teachers and pupils. Any truth which one can find out for oneself is worth a dozen learned by memory.

And yet, there is another side to this coin which says that any fool can learn from experience, but a wise man learns from other peoples' experience. Education must be a combination of these two principles. If one learns only by one's own experience, one may lose much sense of proportion. Mark Twain once observed rather sagely that one should be careful to get out of an experience only the wisdom that is in it and stop there lest he be like the cat that sits down on the hot stove lid; she will never sit down on a hot stove lid again and that's well, but also she will never sit down on a cold one either. The moral, I suppose, is that we should put our mistakes to maximum advantage. Dr. Wilder Penfield has suggested that any great man has made more mistakes than he has achieved successes. There are two differences between a great man and the little man when it comes to mistakes. The great man is not discouraged but puts his faith in God and continues on his quest. Thus he draws the maximum of wisdom from his experience.

I think these points are worth remembering when it comes to implementing our idealism, without which life loses all its purpose.

At the Seventieth Anniversary Dinner, Loyola College, Montreal,
25 March 1966

TO A LARGE EXTENT HOW WELL YOU WILL DO LATER IN LIFE IS BEING DECIDED now by how well you are doing at college. I don't mean only what sort of marks you are obtaining, although they are important also. I mean primarily what lessons you are learning in the art of living.

Whether a person be fit to make his way to the top of any profession in his adult years depends largely upon what he does as a young person to fit himself for the climb. Of course, great efforts are required. These are days when you have to keep running just to keep ahead of the point where your fathers finished their education. World knowledge has increased more perhaps in the last half-century than in all the preceding history of mankind ...

I mentioned to you that marks were important but that other qualities you have learned in school are even more so. One of the first of these is dedication. There is an old Chinese saying: "Great souls have wills; feeble ones have wishes." You must set out a course for yourself in life and pursue it with determination. Certainly if you set no purpose to your life you will find no joy in living and, by extension, the nobler your purpose is, the greater will be your happiness ...

Remember, too, that education does not stop on graduation day. You must go on learning throughout your life if you hope to play a part in a world in which knowledge is expanding so rapidly. Those of you who are undergraduates, remember that the right attitude to learning is something which you can and must develop early in your life. Acquiring an education comes easily to a person who develops a genuine urge to learn. Be curious about everything. Seek to find solutions for problems which puzzle you. If you do this you will find education is not a drudge but an adventure.

Keep your horizons wide and your minds flexible. Remember that everyone you meet knows something that you also could know to your advantage. When you meet people with different points of view, find out what these are and why they were adopted. The better you know people, the more you will understand them, and the more you will like them. If you cherish these attitudes of mind you will be contributing not only to your own maturity but to the unity of our country.

At Lower Canada College, Montreal, 10 June 1966

I BELIEVE THAT THE UNIVERSITY MUST LEAD ITS STUDENTS INTO THE PATHS of the intellect. It must cultivate precision of mind in man in order to enhance his power of conscious thought. We may hope that much that is now automatic or compulsive in our gregarious behaviour will by this means be eliminated ... [Universities] should develop the intellect, the power of analysis and the critical sense in both their teaching staffs and their student bodies. But, you will object, this is not enough, and I would agree with you. For intelligence must be balanced by love if it is to be fruitful in action. By love I mean a power of the will, ready to make choices, based upon a system of values ... The university should provide a setting which will channel nascent ambition and which will direct emergent enthusiasm into action, considered, matured, and thereby fruitful.

I realize that I am asking for a high degree of leadership from the universities. Yet this burden of responsibility must inevitably fall upon those who possess knowledge and the keys to knowledge. The discoveries of today are potentially so dangerous that it is essential that they be put to right use. The academic can no longer afford to retire to his ivory tower. While he should on no account lower his standards, he must keep his feet firmly planted on the ground. The burden of responsibility, which I mentioned, will be the more easily borne if we can produce a race of philosophical scientists and scientific philosophers. Such men should have the breadth of vision to harness the forces latent within mankind in addition to those of the external universe.

On receiving an honorary degree, Laurentian University, Sudbury,
27 October 1961

NO INSTITUTION CAN DEVELOP THIS SENSE OF RESPONSIBILITY AND INVOLVE-ment more readily than can a university. It will be up to our institutions of higher learning to make clear the real values that must guide and dominate the thoughts and actions of good citizens. The university must tap the maximum resources of our young people, the flexibility of their minds, their imagination, their sense of adventure, their zest for living. It must channel these dynamic forces along creative lines towards a sense of responsibility, a sense of commitment to causes greater than themselves, towards a sense of involvement and contribution in the national life of our country. The university must constantly enlarge our horizons, open our minds to the greater good, to the nobler objective, to the more profound meaning and sense of purpose.

At sod-turning ceremony for the St. John Branch of the University
of New Brunswick, 17 May 1966

ONLY TEACHERS OF THE HIGHEST CALIBRE CAN FIRST INSPIRE AND THEN continue to develop the interest of students no matter what their age. Only such teachers can kindle their students' ambition to know more, and then lead them along the path of personal research and creative curiosity ... And when I refer to teachers of the highest calibre, I speak not only of the teach-

ing of technical subjects, but also of the instilling of morality and the edifi-
cation of character. How wisely did Rabelais speak when he declared that
science taught without conscience produces nothing more than the ruination
of the soul.

*During the final conference of the twenty-fifth French language
competitions, Ottawa, 26 April 1962 (translation)*

I WOULD SUGGEST TO YOU THAT AS A GRADUATE ... YOU MIGHT WELL SHOW
two characteristics which seem at first glance to be in conflict: pride and
humility ... Such pride is a grateful pride, and one that will make you want
to give back to your university, your community, and your country the
fullest measure you can of the care and the generosity they have showered
upon you. Such pride is not a boastful, but a quiet pride, as befits a man
who knows that infinitely more has been given to him than he could ever
accomplish with his own resources.

But there is another characteristic that should mark the graduate of ...
any real university. That characteristic is a sincere humility. Never, never
let anyone catch you saying smugly, "Oh, I've been to university," as if
that meant that you had learned all the knowledge in the world. Such an
attitude would only make a wise man wonder if you had learned anything
at all, for the first thing every student should learn at university is a realization of how little, how very very little, he really does know. And the more
one studies, the more one learns, the more this realization should grow.

Even if this were not the case I wonder how many students make the
most of their opportunities at college. Facts which are crammed into one's
brain the day before the examination are liable to be forgotten the day
after; they certainly can't compare with the solid knowledge acquired outside of college by less fortunate folk in honest toil and hard-won experience.
Of course an academic environment *does* provide greater opportunities for
learning, but count only that knowledge really yours that you have firmly
rooted in your memory. An able mind should continue its education as
long and as deeply as it possibly can, but a lazy, complacent, or self-satisfied
one should make way for more worthy recipients.

There is a special responsibility for universities in Canada and their graduates which is of paramount concern. It is the responsibility of making a positive and creative contribution to our sense of purpose and to our unity as a nation.

We have local and regional problems of some importance, and we have, of course, our own personal preoccupations, but I can assure you that there is no question, no problem, no challenge so important to every Canadian today as the unity of our nation; and I believe that universities can if they wish, and must if they value the future of our country, play a decisive role in the achievement of this national unity. I need hardly tell you that no university aware of its responsibilities will retreat into the isolation of ivory towers. The university is an integral part of the national society, and any problem facing the nation must be of concern to it. The university must act as a catalyst in creating an atmosphere of candid, rational, and impartial examination of national problems. It must demonstrate the contribution that historical awareness and exhaustive research can make to discussion. It must exemplify the spirit of the scientific approach to the solving of problems, an approach free of emotionalism, bias, and prejudice. Using all the wisdom and knowledge at their command, universities must guide the great national discussions of our day, and when a conclusion has been reached that is equitable, balanced, and just, the universities must act to implement it to make clear its value; they must use their powers of persuasion and guidance to enlighten public opinion. The universities must preach the indispensability of mutual respect and moderation, and the importance of long-range and national values and interests against short-range profits and local prejudices.

What is the mark of a university graduate when he participates in any discussion? Surely it is the discipline of his intellect as much as his wisdom and his humility. It is the contrast his mind offers with less educated minds; less educated minds which, like blunt weapons, tear and hack instead of cut clean, which lose the point in argument, which cannot comprehend the interests of their adversaries, and which leave the question more obscured and passions more aroused than they found them. I wonder if these distinctions between the educated and the uneducated man are not, to a large extent, also the characteristics which distinguish the positive from the negative protagonists in our contemporary quest for unity.

At Brandon College Convocation, 31 May 1965

PERHAPS MORE THAN AT ANY TIME IN ITS HISTORY, THE WORLD FACES what has been aptly described as the shaking of our intellectual and spiritual foundations. Old patterns of thought have passed away and inevitably their passing has tended to weaken our grasp on the basic values which continue to govern human behaviour. To meet this new and dangerous challenge, equally new and daring innovations must be made ...

If ever the universities of this country begin to believe that education can be achieved by automation, it will mark the decline in the scholastic reputation Canada has.

... [There are] dangers of academic elephantiasis in a large city. As a community grows, there are great pressures placed upon its universities to expand proportionately, but the larger a university becomes, the graver the danger that elephantiasis will set in. This disease is often characterized by a numbness in the affected regions of the body. The outer extremities of the university become so swollen that any intellectual circulation tends to be choked off at its source. The limbs of the university are no longer known to its heart and spirit, and students become no more than mere statistics ...

It may interest you to hear a little story of what elephantiasis can lead to. Not too long ago, in one of our large universities, the students of the Faculty of Law became convinced that the personal relationships between professor and student, which are the essence of spiritual development, were being replaced by anonymity. To prove their point, they enrolled a fictitious character in the Faculty of Law. Charity still existed at that university for when the students told the Bursar that their creation, being poor and a foreign student, was unable to obtain the Canadian currency to pay his fees, the Bursar generously agreed that the student, whose existence he never doubted, could carry on with his studies on credit.

I was told by one of the conspirators that they found a way to complete a paper for him at the examinations. A year passed, and it became only too painfully evident that the nonentity was not only on the way to obtaining a Bachelor of Laws degree, but he might do so with distinction.

The character's sponsors then decided to test the gullibility of their fellow students and they ran their fictitious creation as a candidate for president of the Students' Council. By virtue of a massive publicity campaign, the nonentity was almost elected. But by then the cat could no longer be held in the bag, and word leaked out that a personage considered one of the most promising on campus was, in fact, a figment of his creators' imagination.

It is only with a close personal relationship between the student and his counsellors that a feeling of participation in the university community can be brought to an eager young man and, indeed, participation in the greater community of all seekers of scholastic truth ... the resultant sense of belonging and self-confidence frees new students more quickly from the psychological difficulties of a new environment and permits the development of that self-assurance and maturity necessary to allow him to meet and understand students of different backgrounds, which is one of the most stimulating and rewarding aspects of a university education and one which develops interest, tolerance, and understanding.

The rehumanization of education ... deserves the intellectual support of all Canadians, just as the physical requirements of our academic institutions require our material support. If we in Canada are to achieve cultural and intellectual maturity as a nation, we must match liberality in our attitudes of mind with liberality in our material concern.

The challenge before us is impressive. It remains for us all to seek every way possible to achieve the fulfilment of the destiny intended by Providence for our country.

On opening the new campus of York University, Toronto, 15 October 1965

Knowledge and the Creative Spirit of Man

KNOWLEDGE LEADS TO WISDOM AND WISDOM TO STRENGTH AND PEACE OF mind. Wealth and position may follow on but these are not the most important things. Knowledge makes us more complete, more aware, more tolerant of good and more intolerant of evil.

Message to Canadian Youth, for publication in the fiftieth Anniversary Edition of The Book of Knowledge, *April 1960*

IN ORDER TO LIVE, MEN MUST KNOW. THE AREA AND DEPTH OF THE KNOWLedge demanded of even ordinary men today include not only subjects once reserved to an elite, but also subjects which until recently were not known at all. The application of this fact to the future provides a grave warning to all levels of government and educators. They must prepare our society to meet the great demands that it will certainly encounter. But the matter does not end there. Everyone who has to earn a living must be ready to adapt himself to the changing circumstances of his environment. All of us – and especially students – must seize every possible opportunity to widen continuously the horizons of our learning.

On opening Brock University, St. Catharines, 19 October 1964

A "BOOK" – IN LATIN *liber* – AND PERHAPS IT IS MORE THAN AN ECHO OF the ear that gives us "liberty." The relationship between books and democracy is surely so obvious as to require no elaboration.

An essence of democracy is education, and an essence of education is reading. We are told that "there is nothing to be done which books will not help us to do better"; that "books are the ever-burning lamps of accumulated wisdom" that guide the footsteps of mankind to its future. Thomas Carlyle said that books are "the true university." If this is true for us – the developed, the affluent, the fortunate (to be humble in the appreciation of ourselves) – how much more so must it be true for those struggling to take their rightful place in the sun.

For them, books are like natural resources because the knowledge they contain is essential to the development of natural resources. A gift of a book is a gift of capital, paying dividends each time it is read, to its reader in enlightenment and to its donor in gratitude. The gift of a book is not a momentary kindness but a lasting and recurring thoughtfulness that will be remembered whenever the book is read, so long as its pages hold together.

To students and teachers representing Ottawa high schools which participated in the Students' Overseas Aid Programme of the Overseas Institute of Canada during the International Co-operation Year, at Government House, 2 March 1965

DON'T THINK THAT I AM A GREAT WRITER. I CONFESS, HOWEVER, TO HAVING written two books of speeches. I have no objection to others thinking so!

They were both published during the war. Needless to say, there was only one edition. The following story may help you to judge their value.

When I was in hospital a few years ago there was a very nice charwoman who used to come every day to do the room. We became great friends. One day she said very shyly: "I bought a book today, called *Paroles de guerre*, by somebody called Vanier. Is that you?" I would have liked to deny it but I knew that she would find out anyway. Of course I was very flattered that there was still a demand for the book, so in a moment of vanity I said: "Where did you buy it?" and she replied at a sale in a department store. Remembering that it had been published at about $2.00 I asked her, without thinking, how much she paid for it, and she said, "Seventeen cents."

At Press Gallery Dinner, 20 February 1965

I ONCE SENT A COPY OF A SPEECH I HAD MADE TO A MAN WHO HAD NOT requested it. He replied in a way which I think was polite, but to this day I cannot be sure. He wrote: "Thank you very kindly for the copy of your speech. I can assure you that I shall lose no time in reading it."

At Annual Parliamentary Press Gallery Dinner, Ottawa, 7 May 1966

I WOULD EXPRESS THE HOPE THAT MEMBERS OF THE UNIVERSITY WILL ever recall and ponder the line from Terence "Homo sum, et nil humani alienum a me puto" ["I am a man, and no part of humanity is a stranger to me"]. We live in an age when space is measured in light-years and time in geological aeons. Man therefore appears so small that the temptation arises of considering him only in the mass.

The experience of the horrors that ensue when powerful movements exalt the collectivity to the exclusion of the individual has been with us recently and forcefully. Nevertheless we sometimes close our eyes to these excesses, in the hope that some form of "human engineering" will be able to achieve a new harmony.

I believe that such hopes are all too likely to lead into a blind alley. Should we not rather draw fresh inspiration from the ancient humanities.

The need today is for philosophical scientists and scientific philosophers. Such men should have the breadth of vision to harness the forces latent within mankind in addition to those of the external world. If it be accepted that evolution has taken place and is to continue, surely it must follow increasingly spiritual lines.

I hold that it is the duty of a university to present the sum of human knowledge and culture in a comprehensible form. This form should situate man in his proper context, enabling him to see learning not as a series of isolated fields of specialization but rather as a living whole. Such an organic pattern obviously cannot be exhaustive or it would need to be so encyclopaedic as to require a lifetime of study. Nevertheless it should provide a philosophic base upon which its adepts may found their careers and develop their specialized skills.

On receiving an honorary degree at the University of British Columbia,
20 May 1960

ALL TOO OFTEN [MANY AMONG THE SO-CALLED INTELLECTUALS] ARE SEDUCED by what I might call the positivism of the technique into adopting very one-sided opinions. For example, economic planners will suggest that all will be well with backward peoples once their living standards have been raised. Sociologists will propose systems of human engineering to resolve all our antipathies and frictions. Others will put forward the panacea of world government while the disciples of Marx, Pavlov, and Freud each proclaim methods reflecting their own partial view of the human condition.

Even those who do not adopt a Procrustean explanation of human affairs may be tempted by considerations of efficacy to advocate one solution to the exclusion of all others.

An over-great concern with the human effectiveness of our actions can sometimes lead in two dangerous directions. It may tend towards a pragmatism, which tests truth only by its practical consequences and renders truth at any period relative to the knowledge of the time. Alternatively, such a concern may draw near to Marxism. If this surprises you, remember that Marxism is the outcome of eighteenth and nineteenth century philosophical thought. To the Marxist the only reality is the historical dialectic. He seeks to understand this process and to use its material force with the greatest possible revolutionary effect.

I hope you will not think me a pessimist who has painted a problem-torn world in which the masses are drugged and the presumed leaders enslaved by false doctrines. I do see many rays of hope. In particular I feel that our universities have a major part to play in leading us out of our present darkness. The responsibility of leadership is theirs for they possess knowledge and the keys of wisdom. The academic of today can no longer afford to retire to his ivory tower. His duty is to maintain the highest possible standards in order to lead his students into the paths of the intellect rather than the ways of the passions. He must cultivate precision of mind in order to enhance the power of conscious thought throughout mankind. To this end all faculties must co-operate; they must resolve on mutual comprehension so as to bury the outmoded squabbles that formerly divided scientists and humanists.

Dr. Albert Schweitzer has accused our age, perhaps with justice, of being "filled with disdain for thinking." I hope you will agree that a great mental effort is required to ensure that the "wind of change" shall be a challenge and not a master. We must strive to preserve our intellectual and spiritual conception of man. We must try to generate sufficient mental energy to prevent the loss of our identity, to avoid our absorption in the inchoate mass.

Such an effort should be capable of distinguishing between means and ends. To achieve this it must be based firmly on respect for the truth. Only thus will it be capable of seeing through the mists of propaganda and slanted information in which we live.

At the Fall Convocation of the University of Western Ontario, London,
28 October 1960

I MUST SAY THAT I HAVE THE GREATEST SYMPATHY FOR THE TEACHERS who have to cope with the encyclopaedic amount that is known today. What is more, the boundaries of knowledge are expanding every moment under the impact of our accelerated rate of discovery. In view of this there is bound to be some measure of specialization. Our society is committed to it in order to maintain the momentum of its advance. It is necessary that certain men should sacrifice an all-round competence in their devotion to a skill or vocation, for which they appear to be particularly well suited, while the rest of us should have the widest possible general knowledge. However, even the specialists need a common basis of culture, so that they may exchange ideas, and have interests in common, to prevent them meeting each other like strangers from different planets.

Here parents have a very important part to play, by encouraging their children to read as much as they can while their minds are full of curiosity and their memories still retentive. Without a wide general knowledge, without an active imagination and warm sympathies, it is very difficult indeed for anyone to achieve a satisfactory mental balance. These prerequisites are developed very largely within the home.

At a luncheon of the Canadian Clubs, Hamilton, 21 November 1960

IF A NEOPHYTE MAY BE ALLOWED TO SPEAK TO THOSE WHO HAVE BECOME adepts by their own efforts, I should like to praise the broad-based education which you have always considered necessary for doctors. We are living at a time when specialization becomes every day more necessary and at the same time more potentially dangerous. Happily you realize the need to be specialists and more besides. Therefore you cultivate a warmth of sympathy and an intellectual curiosity which will enable you on occasion to transcend your specialty.

Your vocation is to make use of science, without ever becoming its slave. By its motto *Mente perspicua manuque apta* the College emphasizes the essential balance between physical and spiritual things. May science be your guide but not your master as you walk the tightrope on the border line of these two domains.

Your responsibility will often be great, for as Bacon said, "The greatest trust between man and man is the trust of giving counsel." Yet sometimes you must do more than simply advise. There are times when you have to treat patients without first being able to obtain their consent or their understanding of the remedy you decide upon. In such cases, as indeed at all times, there must be a contact between the whole doctor and the whole patient. The physician must keep in mind the general good of the patient, seeing in him more than simply an opportunity for technical expertise. I am sure that you all act in the spirit of Maimonides when he prayed, "In the sufferer let me see only the human being."

The distinguishing note of the medical profession throughout the ages has been its humanity and its scrupulous regard for truth. Medical ethics are based on a sense of human worth and the practice of healing has been directed towards mankind without regard for religion, nationality, race, or social standing. In the bustle of our century you bear witness to fundamentals that are sometimes overlooked in other walks of life.

To quote Sir Francis Bacon again, "I hold every man a debtor to his profession." All of you here, veterans as well as newly admitted Fellows, are thus in debt, a most honourable debt. I know you will acquit yourselves by service to your fellow-men and by the example you will leave to your successors.

On being made an Honorary Fellow of the Royal College of Physicians and Surgeons of Canada, Ottawa, 20 January 1961

I DON'T MIND TELLING YOU THAT I HAVE BEEN MISTAKEN FOR A MEDICAL doctor once or twice myself because a number of universities have been kind enough to give me an honorary degree of Doctor of Law or Doctor of Military Science. However, I have no illusions that anyone who knows me takes my qualifications very seriously. The other day someone must have telephoned Government House to ask if I were really a doctor because I heard one of my secretaries saying, "Oh, yes, he's a doctor all right, but he's not the sort of doctor that does anybody any good."

At Sixty-Eighth Annual Meeting of the Victorian Order of Nurses, Government House, 6 May 1966

HERE CAN BE CONDUCTED TRAINING IN PSYCHIATRY, PSYCHOLOGY, BIO-chemistry, neurosurgery, and social work; and, also, research in these and other fields to unlock the doors to greater knowledge and to discover undreamed of secrets. One has the impression of a large and powerful and efficient mechanism. One feels the impact of analysis ever carving in upon the unknown. Without really being aware of how it all works, the layman is probably more impressed than any expert would be by the fantastic assortment of equipment gathered here.

All of this is being brought to bear in an inquest upon the human mind which so far has been the recess of personality beyond the reach of other men, open only to the inquiry of conscience and accountable but to God. This been the popular conception but nowadays, wheeling in upon it the tools of an aggressive science, we are to reveal the very nakedness of the mind. In this sense it can be said that with this building and in this institute laymen have licensed the experts to venture in upon the most sacred area of the soul. I can conceive of no more delicate and weighty responsibility.

It seems to me, a layman, that the power of psychiatry must be restrained within a certain morality, and that the keystone of that morality must be constant attention to the power of the spirit. Instances of men overcoming real mental disabilities through the power of the spirit – call it a belief or prayer – are sufficiently common and well documented to form a special field of studies by themselves.

As has been written by the eminent French Nobel Laureate, Dr. Alexis Carrel [*La prière* (Plon, Paris 1944), p. 20]: "Through prayer even the ignorant, the retarded, the weak, the underdeveloped make better use of their intellectual and moral forces. Prayer, it would appear, raises men above the mental stature which normally would be their lot with their heredity and the education they received." He also wrote: "As a physician, I have seen men, after all other therapy had failed, lifted out of disease and melancholy by the serene effort of prayer."

Man is, after all, a human being and though we dissect his personality in the name of science, we must always respect his spiritual values – thus do we set him apart, as we should, from a mere animal. Our aim should ever be the preservation of his humanity.

At opening of the new McGill Training and Research Building of the Allan Memorial Institute, McGill University, Montreal, 13 November 1963

IT IS SAID THAT WE LIVE IN AN AGE OF SPECIALIZATION, THAT BECAUSE MAN has accumulated so much knowledge, it is best for the student to learn a great deal about a very little. This is a process which has been described as the study of more and more about less and less until eventually one knows everything about nothing. I resort to this well-known saying because it underlines one of the great short-comings of the specialist; namely, that frequently his learning is so narrow as to deprive him of the broad knowledge and understanding essential to balanced judgment. According to this classic criticism, the specialist is in fact not an educated man at all. He is one who never learned what to do with a living after he had earned it.

The alternative to the specialist, on the other hand, is supposed to be the man with a broad and balanced education who develops body and mind so as to be generally capable in the world about him. This is the man whom some call a jack-of-all-trades and a master of none. Certainly there is this danger. But, on the whole, it is probably easier for the man with a general background to deepen his knowledge of a particular area than for one who is highly specialized to broaden his.

I suspect that it is this type of thinking that gave rise to the liberal arts colleges ... and, as a graduate of a similar institution, let me say that my experience in life has time and again shown to me the many and varied benefits of this approach, so long as it is taken to heart seriously and its opportunities are fully exploited by the student.

There will be those who say that automation has changed all this, that the complexity of the computer itself demonstrates how even more highly specialized man's learning must become. To those who have not known proper schooling, much less education – and there are in our country many of them – this may be true, but to you who are here today – beneficiaries already of a wide and thorough school system – to you I suggest that automation will mean quite the opposite.

My test is that the personal application of automation to the individual lives of those now students will demand of them a broader and more thorough education than ever before. The machine will soon be able to differentiate and seek out just as the specialist does today, but more accurately, more swiftly, and more persistently than he can ever hope to do. The few examples we see today will be multiplied by thousands. Just as automation seems destined to replace many who now perform simple, repetitious tasks, so also – in craft, muscle, and brain work – computers will soon make obsolete many of those specialists who today command a living solely through their unique control of highly rarefied information. Whatever may have been the case in the past, the world just across the horizon will have no place for the drop-out, the miseducated, the undereducated, and the over-specialized.

R. B. Fuller, the man who invented the geodesic dome and the dymaxion, has said: "The experts do not see any immediate, or even far distant, competition by the machine computer with the human brain in the functions of complex integration." In other words, the machine will remain a machine, and the controlling function of judgment and decision – in the last analysis at least – will remain a human function. Though the rewards are great, the task before mankind is all the more difficult. The world must have educated men more than ever before, and it looks to the universities to provide them ..."

On opening Trent University, Peterborough, 17 October 1964

SCIENTIFIC PROGRESS HAS CREATED GREATER POTENTIALS FOR HUMAN happiness than have existed since man left the Garden of Eden. Diseases and plagues which once destroyed whole populations have now been eradicated or controlled. Technical advances have left man with an unprecedented amount of leisure time and the facilities to enjoy that time. Science has contributed beyond measure towards eliminating many of the sources of suffering and unhappiness which have afflicted man since his creation, and has offered mankind a greater potential for self-fulfilment than he has ever known before, but science by itself cannot bring happiness; no outside force can substitute for something which must come from within.

Our debt to science in physical and material matters is immeasurable. Almost as important has been science's contribution to intellectual values and to the maturity of our society. The scientist contributes clarity of thought, reason before emotion, precision, caution, and integrity to the patterns of thought of his fellow-citizens. The scientific spirit has done much to counter the legacies of superstition and reaction which have been the less fortunate part of our inheritance from previous ages. The scientific approach is one from which every discipline, including the arts, philosophy, and the humanities, can profit. The scientific spirit has sharpened the edge of all our thinking and led to new wisdom in all our mental attitudes.

Perhaps in the long run history will decree that the most important contribution science has made to our present age has been to education, to the removal of prejudices, the widening of horizons, and the more rational use of intelligence.

Examples of the contributions made by the scientific spirit in fields outside of science are too numerous to mention. A very striking one has been in the field of international relations. The forces which divide and separate mankind are not scientific; they are emotional and ideological. The scientific spirit has no use for the irrational elements of these divisions and scientists from any country find they have only to ignore these emotional distractions to be able to talk a common language with like-minded men from any other country. The co-operation, indeed the friendship, established by scientists throughout the world has led in many ways to the creation of a similar climate of mutual respect in non-scientific fields as well. Friendships established by scientists lead to friendships between peoples ...

§ While it is true that science can claim imposing and noble achievements, it cannot at the same time avoid the profound moral responsibilities which these achievements thrust upon it. Left to its own resources, it cannot tell us how to meet these moral responsibilities. Science must be tempered by the humanities. There can be no hope of realizing the full potential of the human spirit if only the scientific side of that spirit is considered important.

When one reads the report of the royal commission on the arts, sciences and humanities, the following question comes to mind. Why should it be necessary for a scientist to have a foundation in the humanities at all? The answer is simply that a foundation in the humanities increases scientific competence. Such a foundation gives the broader viewpoint necessary for the scientist to be able to place his professional objectives in the wider context of life as a whole.

The sad truth is that we tend to lack this breadth of knowledge and understanding. We can reach into the farthest depths of outer space, but we have not yet learned how to see clearly the shallows of the soul. We devote a major portion of our time and energy to the conquest of our environment but the forces of the inner life remain for the most part untapped. I consider that those values and those truths which are eternal are just as important as any theory of relativity.

The new forces unleashed by our scientists in recent years can no doubt be used for our good. But if we are really to control them, we will have to leaven our actions with justice and love.§

At opening ceremonies of the National Research Council's
Fiftieth Anniversary, Ottawa, 21 September 1966

MAN AND ART ARE INTIMATELY RELATED BECAUSE, I AM GOING TO MAKE BOLD to assert, we have been created to the image of God ... By its medium beauty in all its forms – nature, ideas, feelings, or emotions – is conceived and transmitted ...

The civilizing influence of art is such that it might well be one of the answers to our mad rush towards materialism.

At opening of exhibition, Montreal Museum of Fine Arts, 19 January 1960

FOR OVER A CENTURY OUR MAIN TASK HAS BEEN BUILDING. WE HAVE HAD to clear the forests, till the soil, create entire new cities and towns, establish industries, and forge the transportation links that bind one part of the country to the other. We have blasted our way through mountains, stretched bands of steel across the prairies, and dug deep into the ground to produce mineral wealth and oil.

But, amid all this activity, we have had too little time for art and music, literature and drama. Only recently have we begun to realize that with all our tall buildings and our big industries, with all our wheat fields and oil wells and gold mines, something is lacking.

The sum of our material achievements is indeed impressive but it is time we thought of our national heritage in wider terms.

At opening of Exhibition of Graphic Art of the West Baffin
Eskimo Co-operative, Toronto, 4 April 1962

A NATION IS MEASURED PARTLY BY ITS ECONOMIC POWER OR ITS TECHNOlogical competence. However great these may be, it is inevitably the cultural

§Translated from the French.

richness and the creative achievements in the arts for which a civilization is ultimately remembered. A country preoccupied only with material needs is not unlike a man without a soul. Only in the expression of spiritual or aesthetic values can a nation find true maturity and enduring wealth.

Of all the creative arts, the theatre is the one which perhaps most closely can capture the spirit of a nation and involve those associated with it in a greater awareness, not only of themselves, but also of ultimate reality. The theatre can help us refocus our thoughts on the beautiful and the significant aspects of our lives. It can restore to us the perspective we need to appreciate what is of lasting value – a perspective we must have to become worthy citizens and mature individuals.

Message for the Dominion Drama Festival Programme, May 1966

MUSIC IS A COMMON MEDIUM OF EXPRESSION, AVAILABLE TO ALL THE peoples of the world no matter what differences of language may otherwise divide them. Because of this universality, music, particularly folk music, has the potential to make a real contribution to mutual understanding and peace among the nations. At the same time, such folk music gives expression to each country's distinctive cultural characteristics, making known as no other medium of expression can the true heart and soul of a nation's people.

To the International Folk Music Council, 3 September 1961 (translation)

THE LITERATURE OF A COUNTRY IS A GOLDEN CHAIN THAT GIVES THE people of that country their place and continuity in time. So long as it flourishes there is an assurance of spiritual as well as material development, of substantial as well as superficial national progress.

To recipients of the Governor-General's Awards for Literature,
24 April 1964

THE IMPORTANCE OF YOUR CONTRIBUTION TO THE LIFE OF A NATION IS far-reaching and richly deserves recognition and appreciation. To you is given this gift, the magic which permits escape into posterity.

While we, ordinary men, may fear the power of your judgment, may beg of you direction in our weary way, we at least are spared the burden of responsibility which you must forever carry ...

Of you is required truth, understanding, and charity. Gifted above all men you may be, but as from those to whom much is given, much is required, so upon you do we depend for the look-out's cry of warning, for the wise man's explanation of meaning, for the scribe's telling of our story to our children and our children's children.

On presenting the 1961 Governor-General's Awards for Literature,
2 April 1962

THE THEATRE PRESENTS US ALL – PARTICIPANT AND SPECTATOR ALIKE – with an opportunity for instruction as well as entertainment. Whatever the tale, it is a commentary on life, told in a manner which will always remain man's most vivid and powerful method of telling a story. The theatre shows mankind to itself.

In its function the theatre cannot avoid having substantial moral, social, and political impact. It reflects the beliefs of its creators, the traditions of their origin, and the state of their society. As such, it becomes a valuable element both in national development and in mutual understanding, functioning best and contributing most fully when in all its aspects it springs freshly from native soil.

Message for the Souvenir Programme of the Dominion Drama Festival,
May 1962

SOME WOULD SEE IN OUR TWO LANGUAGES, IN OUR PROXIMITY TO GREAT and powerful nations, insuperable obstacles to originality in these developments. I would suggest rather that these factors present a unique and wonderful opportunity to create a fresh, authentic contribution to the theatre and literature of both French- and English-speaking traditions.

Message for the Dominion Drama Festival Souvenir Programme, May 1963

The Nation

The Challenge of Unity

CONFEDERATION WAS NOT THE STARTING-POINT OF OUR HISTORY, WHICH stretches back much further than that. It could be better described as a landmark along our path to nationhood. For those who conceived of a united country, who explained their idea to the people, and who finally gave constitutional form to their idea, Confederation was a great act of faith. We see it now as a constructive attempt to live with and gradually dominate the problems of history and geography. These problems may once have seemed well-nigh hopeless. They have been reduced and made manageable by a century of national life, shaped and guided by a common purpose derived from the inspiration of the Founding Fathers.

If some of the original problems have been eliminated, this, however, does not mean that we face the prospect of plain sailing in a stormless sea. The very solution of old difficulties has often produced a crop of new ones. Problems also have a habit of changing shape, so that what was yesterday a ques-

tion of economics becomes today a matter of psychology and personal understanding. At the present time we have no dearth of difficulties or lack of
problems to tax our ingenuity and our goodwill – without speaking of the
tax on our pockets ... I should like to suggest that what we need as we
grapple with our actual situation is a spirit of national maturity. I feel that
such a spirit could be the spring-board for a great new leap forward. It
could provide a stimulus and a starting-point comparable to that of 1867.

Let me therefore try to explain what I mean by maturity. We often use
the term when speaking of young people growing up. A boy, for example,
begins by acquiring factual knowledge; to this he must add understanding.
One then hopes that gradually with time and experience he will attain
wisdom, which shows itself in mature judgment. Maturity is thus something
affecting the whole personality. It implies a balance, a degree of self-con-
sciousness and a sense of responsibility. I believe that this concept can be
applied to the nation at large. We must strive to produce a people that is
not dependent, which realizes its weaknesses just as much as its strength,
which is therefore capable of setting its own goals in the light of self-
knowledge.

It will be no easy task to ensure that all the components of the mosaic of
Canada's population take part in this process of growing up. The problem
of full participation is complicated by the rapid rhythm of change built into
the century in which we live. Statesmen have generally had to apply to the
questions of their day the training which they received in their youth, perhaps a generation or even longer beforehand. This necessary time-lag between preparation for and attainment of high office was of little moment
in more stable times. Today it demands a great effort of adaptation from
those responsible for major decisions. Now too, even the rank and file have
to undergo the mental gymnastics of adjusting their minds to the infinite,
and of accustoming themselves to measure space by light-years and time by
geological epochs.

These personal difficulties should not, however, be allowed to blind us to
the demands that the cause of national maturity will make on each and
every one of us. One of the greatest needs of the moment is for a more active
and widespread civic spirit. We must take pride in our communities and refuse to tolerate injustice and inefficiency within them. Edmund Burke once

remarked: "All that is necessary for the triumph of evil is that good men do nothing." And one of the leaders in Canadian industry asked, only the other day: "Are enough Canadian corporations and businessmen accepting their responsibility and grasping their opportunity to participate in public affairs? Are there enough Canadians whose sense of responsibility will lead them to share in the democratic process?" For democracy is a challenge to all. Active democrats must have faith that their fellow-citizens love and seek the common good. It is up to us not to disillusion them. We must prove our zeal for the common good, which is above individual interests, by standing firm for justice and truth even at the cost of personal sacrifices. If we can spread this attitude we shall find that the law will be obeyed because it is seen to involve the common good. It will be kept even when it could safely be broken for the sake of private gain.

Civic spirit originates at the parish or community level; as it rises higher it blends imperceptibly with patriotism. Now patriotism I would describe as a mature form of nationalism. The patriot is "for" his country without being "against" anyone else. He does not condemn other nations, neither does he make excuses for his own country. He is a level-headed realist who believes that his people have something worth while within them to give. All too often in the past, I am sorry to say, we in Canada have been apt to alternate between a narrow nationalism and a facile rejection of our own efforts and even of our own successes. Let us try to cultivate a balanced view, let us avoid the temptation to seek a sensational headline when we discuss our own country.

Patriotism by itself, however, is not enough. We are called upon today to have an international outlook. Self-interest even dictates this, for Canada lives by its foreign trade. Over and above our commercial relations with the world, we have been gifted with a dual culture originating overseas while at the same time innumerable ties of kinship link us to Europe and to the United States. The role which we can and must play within the family of the Commonwealth is yet another reason for turning our gaze outwards. The new uncommitted nations which are emerging throughout the world likewise demand our attention. I wonder what proportion of Canadians realize that we cannot isolate ourselves in our particular ivory tower. How many understand that other people's problems are our problems? We cannot consider ourselves to have attained national maturity until the extent of our involvement in the world is widely grasped ...

You may perhaps feel that I have located the spirit of national maturity at a rather remote level. I hope I have not given the impression of preaching something which is only important in moments of national or international crisis. Maturity is an attitude of mind which we can never afford to lay aside. It is something which must be with us from day to day in all the complexities of family and social living. It must be our guide in dealing with such specific problems as crime, juvenile delinquency, alcoholism, drug addiction, mental ill-health, or the break-up of families. These are scourges which the normal family and community hope and pray will never touch them. Yet even if we are spared, we still remain, each to some extent, our brother's keeper. Therefore we cannot abdicate all responsibility and simply leave it to government to look after the victims. In circumstances where prevention is so much more effective than treatment, it is essential to mobilize the energies of the whole community.

The whole community must take part in the effort to achieve maturity. It can do so by raising its standards and improving the quality of its life. Our language, our thought, our use of time both in work and in leisure, all of these must bear the stamp of quality. Only by excelling in whatever she does will Canada win for herself the respect of nations.

Having tried to outline some of the fields in which national maturity would naturally operate, I should now like to consider means by which a mature outlook might be stimulated. I believe that we need to develop within us the power of vision, that is to say, the ability to see things as they really are. We must liberate ourselves from prejudices and try to avoid seeing the problems of today with the eyes of yesterday. In this context I believe that philosophy is of prime importance. For not only does it condition to some extent the eyes of the beholder but it also determines the behaviour of those he is observing. The actions of men reflect their thinking. Let us take into account their ultimate aims just as much as immediate motives. I suggest that it is the duty of mature citizens to open wide the eyes of the mind, allowing them to range freely outside the field of day-to-day business.

The sequence examine, judge, act is, I think you will agree, a logical one, leading us to sensible conclusions. I have touched on the first step, examination. As for the second, judgment, it is rare for us to be able to judge *in vacuo* without knowing at all what will be the consequences of our judgment. I suggest that in all questions touching on national maturity we need a sense of direction. It is sometimes said that politics is the art of the possible and that all problems are not capable of rapid solution. I agree, but I hold that unless we have a clear purpose in mind, we shall never even know what is possible. If we are content to drift, we shall never achieve anything ...

I am sure that it is essential for all those not debarred by office to formulate their own opinions and express them vigorously. As a stimulus, how useful is a grain or two of discontent, above all when it is of the creative sort. A little discontent can shatter complacency and urge us to non-conformity, making us dissatisfied with what we know already. Under its impulse we can resist the mass pressures and the hidden persuaders, and seek always to expand the limits of the private world we know.

Notes for remarks at a luncheon of the Empire Club, Toronto,
9 February 1961

YOU HAVE UNDERSTOOD THE IMPORTANCE OF FRENCH CULTURE IN THE world, the benefits which it can bring, the essential role that it plays here in your immediate neighbourhood. You are right in wishing to understand French culture.

In the Middle Ages and during the Renaissance, France, through her cathedrals and her poets, played a preponderant part in our Western world. And, in order to understand our modern world, to grasp its deepest aspirations, its need for justice and liberty, whether in anguish or revolution, is it not in France that we should seek its origins and principal initiators? The French language, coming as it does from Latin and Greek, offered a unique means of expression, of clear and orderly analysis, and so, of universal communication. Over the centuries France has added to its wealth through a history which, while no doubt playing a military, political, and economic part of the highest importance, exercised to an even greater extent a spiritual influence on the world through its artists, philosophers, and saints.

The mutual knowledge of our two languages and of our two cultures will help us to understand the respective histories of France and of Great Britain. Are they not to some extent one and the same history? From the general point of view, how can we possibly separate these two countries which, almost always, are to be found together in the same military, scientific, diplomatic, and economic fields? According to the time or place, one precedes the other, but in most cases the second one immediately reappears as a competitor or as a protagonist. The history of these two countries is the same, but seen from two different angles according to the two different but complementary genii. If these two great nations have come up against one another so frequently in the past, either on a battle-field or in a race to explore some unknown universe, or to extend their respective empires, was it not because they both had the same sense of universality and the same noble and magnanimous will to spread civilization?

The world will not find peace, except through the harmonization of the universe as a whole. France and England – countries which in history and geography represent the world at middle age – retain an essential role and it is this that explains the spiritual destiny of our country. By her geographical and historical situation, Canada, if it wishes, can have a leading role to play in the conciliation of other nations, in the effort to bring together all men of good faith for the realization at last of a unity that will permit every man in every country to have a human existence in justice and in peace here on earth.

So it is that English-speaking and French-speaking Canadians must know one another and understand one another in order that they may continue the long tradition of Anglo-French civilization.

Rudyard Kipling expressed the same thought in the following terms at the Sorbonne in November 1921: "For thirty generations, France and England in secular but fruitful conflict have engendered and sustained a civilization which has been attacked by an immense and highly organized barbaris ..."

In this joint secular work, France has made an immense contribution to the heritage of the moral, spiritual, and civilizing forces of humanity. In fact, the world is her debtor. Her culture has enlightened and enriched it for centuries.

These are some of the reasons, taken from history, which should incite

Canada to know and to understand France. I would add another. French culture was the first element of civilization planted in Canada. Nothing can change the historic fact that during two hundred years it was the only one in the country. Many Canadians are unaware of its existence because of their distance from the centre of this culture, but it exists in abundance, and has made in cultural affairs a prodigious progress during the past few years. I will not offend you who know how important it is by an enumeration of its many manifestations. They are so numerous in the fields of literature, painting, sculpture, music, the theatre, and the dance, that I might run the risk of omitting some ...

And this culture goes back a long time. Because of my forebears, anything I say about French culture in Canada might be thought biased, so I shall quote the testimony of a few of my predecessors.

Here is what Lord Dufferin said in Quebec in 1878:

It is needless for me to assure you with what pleasure I again find myself taking part in those refined and artistic relations with which the French race delight to solace their leisure ... It has been one of the happy peculiarities of your nationality that you have ever known how to enliven the serious occupations of life by a graceful gaiety and to introduce a brilliancy of colour amid the sombre shadows of our dull work-a-day world. This happy temperament not only sheds its benign influence over your social existence, but it has invested everything you have touched – your architecture, your literature, your history – with a most attractive individuality. Brilliancy, picturesqueness, dramatic force, a chivalrous inspiration – these are the characteristics which have thrown over the annals of Canada a glamour of romance which attaches to the history of no other part of the continent ...

Your past has refused to die. Its vitality was too exuberant, too rich with splendid achievements, too resonant, too replete with the daring and gallantry of stately seigneurs – the creations of able statesmen – the martyrdoms of holy men and women, to be smothered by the dust of ages, or overwhelmed by the uproar of subsequent events.

The Marquess of Lorne, on his arrival in Quebec in 1879, said in French:

J'exprime ces sentiments dans cette belle langue qui, dans tant de pays et durant des siècles fut regardée comme le type de l'expression concise et nette et le plus habile interprète de l'esprit et de la pensée humaine.

Le monde entier en l'employant, se rappelle avec vous que c'est la langue qui, dans l'église, se répandit avec éloquence des lèvres de Saint Bernard et de Bossuet; et qui, avec Saint Louis, Du Guesclin et l'héroïque Pucelle d'Orléans résonna sur les champs de bataille.

... Ne fut-ce pas de Québec que les paroles de foi, les impérissables richesses de la science et de la civilisation se répandirent à travers un nouveau continent ?[1]

Lord Tweedsmuir, at Quebec, speaking to the Congrès de la langue française in June 1937, declared in French:

Le Canada a le bonheur de posséder deux des grandes traditions de l'Europe, la française et l'anglaise. Vous avez conservé votre langue, votre droit, votre religion, et votre culture si riche d'histoire, d'un si grand prix pour le Canada tout entier. Votre langue surtout est un bien précieux, car la langue et la littérature françaises constituent une richesse non seulement pour le Canada français mais encore pour le Canada anglais.[2]

Still speaking in French, he added:

Votre poésie, qui exprime si bien l'âme d'un peuple, m'a profondément intéressé. Mais le Canada français ne fait que commencer son œuvre littéraire. Il réunit tous les éléments d'une grande littérature – un peuple dont l'histoire est l'une des plus romanesque qui soient, une paysannerie qui heureusement a su rester proche du terroir et conserver ses vieilles traditions. Je prévois que le Canada français collaborera avec distinction à ces travaux de l'esprit qui resteront toujours à la

---

[1] "I am expressing these sentiments in that beautiful language which, in so many countries and during so many centuries, was considered as the prototype of a clear and concise expression of man's feelings and the best interpreter of human thought.

  The whole world, when it makes use of it, remembers as you do that it is the language which, in the Church, was used with eloquence by Saint Bernard and Bossuet and that it was used on the battle-field by Saint Louis, Du Guesclin and the Maid of Orleans.

  ... Was it not from Quebec that the inestimable treasures of religion, science and civilization spread throughout the New World?"

[2] "Canada has been fortunate to inherit two great European traditions: the French and the English. You have retained your language, your laws, your religion and your culture, so rich in history and so precious for the whole of Canada. Your language especially is a priceless gift, for French language and literature constitute a wealth not only for French-speaking Canada but for English-speaking Canada as well."

base de la civilisation véritable, car il participe à deux grandes traditions, la française et l'anglaise.[3]

Such testimonies show that Canada has long been a centre of French culture. In time it will become, I have no doubt, truly a genuine source of this culture and will thus make an essential contribution to the development and to the heritage of French genius.

Why should Canada have a special affection for France? In the first place, because it was the French who founded Canada; their presence is felt everywhere. Their roots are thrust deep in the earth. The first to leave their imprint were the martyrs, the discoverers, the settlers. These pioneers not only penetrated Canada but the United States also. Knowing our history as you do, I am sure that I need not recall the travels of Champlain, Brulé, Nicolet, Radisson, Groseillers, Albanel, Joliet, Marquette, La Salle, La Vérendrye, who explored North America from Hudson Bay to the Gulf of Mexico and to the foot-hills of the Rockies.

Addressing French Canada at Montreal on the 21st November 1872, Lord Dufferin declared in French:

Brave et noble race qui la première fournit à l'Europe les moyens d'importer la civilisation sur le continent d'Amérique. Race valeureuse et hardie dont les explorateurs dans l'intérieur de ce continent ont permis à l'industrie européenne de s'implanter non seulement sur les bords du Saint-Laurent mais encore dans les riches vallées de l'Ohio et du Mississippi; les premiers forts qu'elle érigea et les premiers établissements qu'elle forma sont devenus aujourd'hui grâce au jugement droit et à l'espèce d'instinct qui la caractĕrise, le noyau de grandes villes et de puissantes populations; et c'est à leur coopération actuelle et à leur intelligence naturelle que nous devons une bonne partie de la condition prospère de cette province.[4]

3 "Your poetry, which expresses the soul of a people so well, has deeply impressed me. French Canada is only just starting on its literary career. It combines all the elements of a great literature – a people whose history is one of the most romantic to be found, and a peasantry which has fortunately remained in close contact with the soil and preserved its ancient traditions. I foresee French Canada taking part and distinguishing itself in those achievements of the mind which will always constitute the basis of true civilization, for it shares two great traditions, the French and the English."

4 "A brave and noble race which was the first to provide Europe with the means of importing civilization to the American continent. A valorous and fearless nation

Another reason for Canada to have a special affection for France, and for France to have a special affection for Canada, is that there has been an extension of Canada into France. In the course of two great wars 110,000 Canadians gave their lives. In so far as it has been possible for me to establish, 50,000 of these lie buried in France. These are striking figures, which reveal the vigour, the valour, and the courage of Canadians. Only a country which possesses these qualities can make such an effort despite a sparse population. No, Canada, with so many of her children over there, cannot renounce her intimate friendship with France. The dead and the living are but one in the narrow and profound communion of the nation.

Each of us carries the hope of those who have gone and those who are yet to come. Upon each of us is incumbent the duty to keep the sacred fire which, across the ages, has enlightened and inspired men who adhere faithfully to the principles of truth, of justice, and of charity ...

We have already said that the annals of history record the glory and the renown of Great Britain and of France. The future of Canada is intimately allied to this fabulous double heritage. I hope and pray that Canadians of Anglo-Saxon and French descent, whose two cultures are a source of mutual enrichment, will be an example of fraternal coexistence, and that they will advance hand in hand to make of Canada a great nation, hand in hand also with Canadians of all origins, without distinction of race or creed, with their languages and their cultures. We are all God's children.

At inauguration of the programme of French-Canadian Studies at McGill University, Montreal, 26 November 1963

FRANCE AND CANADA, ALTHOUGH SITUATED IN QUITE DIFFERENT REGIONS of the world, are guided by the same sense of human values and share the same ancient heritage. Bonds of common blood, common spirit, and com-

---

whose explorations into the hinterland of this continent enabled European industry to take root not only on the shores of the St. Lawrence, but also in the rich valleys of the Ohio and Mississippi; through the sound judgment and the instinct that characterize [its members], the early forts they erected and the first settlements they established have today become the nucleus of large cities and powerful populations; and it is to their present co-operation and natural intelligence that we owe a good part of the prosperous state of this province."

mon heart unite both countries, bonds which have been strengthened in the heat of battle, strengthened in the struggle to preserve a common patrimony not only material but spiritual. These bonds between us can and must develop freely in an atmosphere of peace and brotherhood.

What is the mission of French Canadians if it is not to carry on the French tradition and through it the tradition of the entire Latin civilization? Our call is to demonstrate this inheritance among people whose culture is far removed from that of France ...

How can French Canada best fulfil this mission? The existence of a separate French identity in Canada has already been assured. It is an established fact which nothing can change. But the *quality* of this French fact has not yet been determined. This quality depends on us, above all on the rising generation among us upon whom will fall the imperative duty of enriching French life in Canada, of refining it, humanizing it, and augmenting its spiritual content. In the past, we have had to insist on our survival as a distinct people. Now that this survival is assured, let us fight equally hard to guarantee its worth. We can do so, if only we have the will to make the required effort. With determination and hard work we can acquire the excellence we need to rise above mediocrity and guarantee genuine success. Indeed, with the universities we possess, we have the potential for creating standards which will be of really transcendent value.

To achieve this excellence of which I speak we will continue to draw on the well-springs of our culture in France. But it is my hope that, in due time, French Canada will become in its own turn a genuine source of French culture. The University of Montreal serves as a link between French Canada and the other French-language universities throughout the world. In so doing it bears living witness to the richness and the universality of French culture. As did Greek in the Middle East and Latin in Western Europe in olden times, the French language and French culture today provide invaluable tools for achieving understanding and promoting unity among the nations of the world. French thought brings to those skilled in its use the spiritual values which are so desperately needed in this present age. It provides the inspiration of a humanism which stresses personal worth and dignity. It offers to us the promise of a most rewarding exchange of mutual enrichment.

But because it is an *exchange* which is offered, a certain duty is imposed upon us. After having received so much for so long, it is now our turn to make our own contribution to French thought. We should begin by acting as its interpreter to our English-speaking compatriots in Canada, many of whom yearn for the widening of their horizons which the knowledge of a second language offers.

It is wrong to suggest that we can have only one culture if we want strength and unity in our country. We should never forget that biculturalism has been used as a powerful cohesive force by some of the most far-flung empires in history, from the Manchu dynasties in China to the Roman Empire in the West. In spite of their military and technological superiority over the other peoples of the Mediterranean, if the Romans had contented themselves with merely winning battles they could never have founded both an empire and a civilization. They had to bind that empire together with the bilingual and bicultural association of the Greek and Latin civilizations. The Romans had to assmilate Greek culture completely. Their elite had to learn to speak Greek fluently and to use the language in their administration of the countries of Africa and the Near East.

In the world of tomorrow, biculturalism will perhaps provide Canada's greatest opportunity. No other country in the world has a comparable potential. If we, as Canadians, neglect a chance so priceless, history will never forgive us.

At the University of Montreal, 11 December 1965 (translation)

IN THE CLOUDS WHICH DARKEN THE SKIES OF OUR TIME, A DOUBLE SIGN OF hope seems to break through and to become ever clearer: the desire for unity and for peace.

All men feel an increasing conscious and resolute need to reach unity; they seem more and more desirous to forget their past quarrels with their blunders and errors, and to be ready to make real sacrifices to carry out God's commandment.

Men of goodwill in all countries and of all religions are eager to establish on earth a peace real and lasting, based on justice, truth, and love. Our world is becoming more and more conscious that true peace requires first a spiritual disarming, the expulsion from our hearts of any feeling of hate, jealousy, violence. Outer peace involves first a unity of hearts and souls.

The cry for unity in Canada is great. It is inconceivable that the heirs to the two great Western civilizations – Anglo-Saxon and French – should be unable to find a brotherly way of life based upon respect for rights conferred by history, a respect also for conventions freely accepted nearly a century ago but adapted to the exigencies of our time.

New Year's Message, 1964

IF ONE LOOKS BENEATH THE SURFACE, ONE FINDS THAT MANKIND IS UNITED in appreciation of the essential values of life and in recognition of the wisdom and power which are to be derived from diversity. If we were all alike, there would be no mutual inspiration or sense of competition to spur our creative capabilities. Differences between men are necessary for without them we would have no basis on which to compare our thoughts and our assumptions, nor any yardstick to measure our goals and our achievements. It is a wise man who realizes the richness of diversity ...

Our gain as individuals is also our nation's gain. I admit it's a little daring for a country to count on drawing its strength from diversity. It's much easier perhaps to talk of a melting-pot and to force everyone to behave alike; how much simpler could we fashion our national and international policies as a country if all our people were the same dull shade of grey! But how much more shallow, how much less sensitive and understanding would such policies be! No, if we *can* draw our strength from diversity, the result will be more considerate and compassionate than any force drawn from mediocre conformity.

At a luncheon, Winnipeg, 29 May 1965

EACH PROVINCE, EACH CITY, EACH NEIGHBOURHOOD, AND EVEN EACH HOME in Canada has something of which to be proud. Ours must be a constructive pride which sees our place in the greater whole. There is no room for selfish vanity or petty regionalism. I do not wish to be known as a citizen of any province or of any city. I wish to be known as a citizen of Canada. No man is an island to himself, and no region in this country can reach even a fraction of its full potential if it sticks its head in the sand like an ostrich and imagines that it can get along without the rest of Canada. The prosperity of any part of Canada cannot be separated from the prosperity of the whole, and the spirit of our country, if it is to amount to anything, is equally indivisible. If we place our primary loyalties in some local group or region, we will become a collection of minor principalities, no single one of which could be taken seriously by the rest of the world. If, on the other hand, we give our first and foremost patriotism to Canada, we will build a nation which will be respected and envied everywhere.

I am an optimist. I believe that we can, and will, fulfil the future that God has intended for us, but I know, and I am sure you will agree with me, that we will reach this future only if we remain united, only if our first loyalty remains firmly and forever to our country as a whole.

What then are some practical ways to promote this unity which is so important for our country? Firstly I would say that unity depends on an attitude of mind. We must be young in spirit if we are to match the youthfulness of our country. What is one of the most endearing qualities of a young person's mind? Surely it is his eagerness to learn, his willingness to study things that are new and different, his freedom from the prejudice and bias which prevent him from absorbing new knowledge and reaching new wisdom. This is the attitude that we all must have towards the differences in our points of view and in our ways of life. Let us not be afraid of things that are new to us, or retreat into our shells like hermit crabs. Let us remember that every new outlook, every different way of doing things, has something to teach us, something of value for us to learn. Wisdom is an accumulation of many steps of knowledge, from many different sources. Let us remain young in spirit and eager to learn.

Secondly, and this is an even more specific suggestion, I wonder if we would not all be wise to add a second language to our own, whatever it may be. The very learning of another language gives one a new appreciation of one's own, a new awareness of its richness and possibilities, and a knowledge of new forms of expression and flexibility which will not only improve our spoken word, but the flexibility of our mental processes as well.

But knowledge of another tongue brings much more than this. Many of you will no doubt have read of Jules Verne's suggestion that the centre of our earth is hollow and that there is another world within our globe which we have only to dig down to reach. Learning another language is a bit like discovering such a world. We suddenly burst out on a whole new universe of literature of great thoughts. The new opportunities presented to us are almost as startling as new horizons which opened to us when we first learned how to read our own language.

Wherever we have travelled in western Canada we have been impressed not only with the material achievements we have seen, but also with the progress which has been made in cultural development. Surely this learning of a second language is an essential requisite to our cultural maturity. In Europe no man is considered educated unless he has mastered at least one tongue other than his own. It used to be that Canada was so isolated by physical distances that we could afford the parochialism of speaking only one language. Nowadays, however, events anywhere in the world are liable to make their influence felt at once in our country; our destiny has suddenly become closely linked with that of other nations, and the speed of modern transportation and communication has brought the four corners of the world as close to each of us as our next door neighbour. We need vitally to be able to talk to these new neighbours, to understand them, and to have them understand us. This is an age of bitter competition in the export not only of goods but also of ideas. We must be equipped to hold our own in the market-places of the world, and we cannot expect to do so unless we first achieve our own cultural maturity.

These comments on the wisdom of learning another language have already led me to a third practical way to ensure the unity and the greatness of this country, for as quickly as we learn another language we come to know as well the people who speak that language. I once met an old lady who seemed to me at first to be rather dim-witted. "I declare," she said, "I do not like such and such a people." "Do you know these people well?" I asked her, and then she showed much more wisdom than I had credited her with, for she replied: "Of course I do not know them at all. How could I dislike them if I knew them!"

I have spoken before of the virtues that lie in variety. We have much to learn from each other. No one people have a monopoly on wisdom or happiness. Each of us can enrich his own life immeasurably by drawing on the experience and knowledge of others, and quite apart from the new dimensions such learning adds to our own lives, it brings the finest bonus of all, affection and mutual esteem. To appreciate another person inevitably leads to being appreciated, and to appreciate is to understand; to understand is to love.

Notes for remarks at a civic luncheon, Edmonton, 3 June 1965

I WONDER ... IF I MIGHT SUGGEST THAT A HAPPY CHOICE FOR A SECOND language might be French. For many years I have been telling my French-speaking compatriots of the boundless advantages for them in learning English. I have told them of the need to know and understand their fellow-Canadians who speak English. I have told them that the only hope for the unity of this country is to be found in the ability of our two minds to meet as one.

I wonder now if I could extend these counsels that I have been giving to my French-speaking friends, and suggest them for the consideration of my English-speaking compatriots ...

Even if there were not a single French-speaking person in Canada, consider for a moment the wealth that lies in the heritage of French words. The French language embodies the achievements of fifteen centuries of civilization, some of the greatest philosophers, theologians, and writers in the history of the world. More Nobel prizes have been awarded for literature to French writers than to those of any other nationality.

For centuries French has been a language of artistic expression. It has also been the diplomatic language of the world. Even today international treaties between two non-French-speaking countries are often drawn up in a French version as well. French is the first language of three countries and the second language of more than a score of others. If Canadians are to compete in the markets of the world, if we are to win friends and influence others to our way of thinking abroad, then a good knowledge of French is a requirement. And even if we never travel abroad ourselves, the ease with which ideas are exchanged in this modern age allows us all as it were to become spiritual citizens of the world. We could not, I submit, consider ourselves to be such citizens or indeed think that our education had been complete or that our wisdom had reached its cultural maturity until the abundance and the luxuriance of the French language were ours. These are reasons, as I have mentioned, which would suggest that a knowledge of French, every bit as much as a knowledge of English, would be a requisite for a fully educated man, even if there were not in Canada one person speaking the language as his own.

But in fact I need hardly remind you that we have a very much alive and very dynamic French fact in this country. The resurgence of French self-awareness and creativity is surely one of the most startling and impressive phenomena in the contemporary world.

French Canada wants to fulfil the promise of its own civilization, and to do so it has mobilized a galaxy of devoted talent. French-Canadian literature, art, poetry, politics, journalism, and indeed every aspect of self-expression is enjoying a surge of the spirit that is electrifying even the humblest Québecois. What we are witnessing in French Canada is perhaps as talented and as purposeful an outburst of creative energy as can be found anywhere. English-speaking Canadians should be proud of this rebirth of French-Canadian culture. It is a superb achievement enhancing all of us.

But we can do much more than merely admire this renaissance in French Canada. We can become a part of it. We can share its new discoveries. We can enjoy with it its new spiritual insights, and we shall find, if we do so, that we are enriching our own lives in more than a mere abstract or aesthetic way. As we come to appreciate and enjoy the beauties of this flowering of French self-expression, we shall come to know and relish the distinctive qualities of the people who are part of it, and in understanding, we will be understood ourselves, and in liking we will be met with equally warm affection.

Notes for remarks at a state dinner given by the Lieutenant-Governor of Alberta, Edmonton, 4 June 1965

WHEREVER I WENT IN WESTERN CANADA MY MESSAGE WAS A SIMPLE ONE, and it was always the same: that this country has the most wonderful future in the world if only it remembers the importance of unity. I emphasized that unity can only come through understanding. I was asked for specific suggestions and in Edmonton I said that just as I had always urged my

French-speaking compatriots to learn English, so my English-speaking compatriots could make a concrete contribution to the unity of our country by learning French.

I found a great desire on the part of westerners to hear about the situation in Quebec, much goodwill, no bitterness, only a need for information. We must remember that the eastern border of Quebec is closer to Paris than it is to Victoria. It is not surprising that without some rational explanation of the sudden French renaissance it is difficult for them to understand what is happening in French-speaking Canada. Frankly I feel that more spokesmen, English- as well as French-speaking, should go west to help interpret French aspirations just as westerners should come to Quebec ...

In this country we have a very much alive and very dynamic French fact. The resurgence of French self-awareness and cultural creativity is surely one of the most impressive phenomena in the contemporary world. French Canada wants to fulfil the promise of its own culture and to play fully its role as an equal and respected partner in the great Canadian experiment. To do so, French-speaking Canadians have brought to the fore their leading men of talent in every field – writers, artists, poets, journalists, social scientists, and scholars. We should all be happy at the rebirth of French culture which enriches all Canadians.

The fact that my remarks in this vein were carried by newspapers throughout western Canada, and were favourably commented on, suggests that there is a willingness and even an eagerness, as I said before, among western Canadians to learn more of and to understand the changes which are under way in French-speaking Canada. It is such understanding that is essential to a country which has based its hopes and expectations on obtaining strength through diversity.

We all, I think, have some inkling of this country's natural resources: I have said before that if we were to add up only our known resources and divide by our population we would almost certainly discover that we were, per capita, the richest nation in the world. But I wonder if we realize as well the quality of our *human* resources. I have served Canada for twenty-five years in foreign countries, and I can assure you that there is no nation more highly thought of overseas.

I cannot emphasize too strongly the contributions made by all the settlers from whatever land, at whatever time, who have come and are coming to Canada. It is true that most of them arrived with little material wealth; but they had much more essential gifts to offer: they had imagination, they had initiative, they had adaptability, and they had common sense and a desire to work. What kind of people came to Canada? The best! The ones with the ability to throw off the shackles of an old and circumscribed way of living, with the intelligence to realize the potential of a new life, and with the sense of adventure to achieve it.

In Canada we are proud of our diverse characteristics. The heritage and traditions of our forefathers have been built and cherished through the centuries; they are too valuable to be abandoned in favour of any rigid uniformity. To suggest that we forget the richness and wisdom that each of our peoples has brought to Canada, in favour of some sort of artificial cultural common denominator, would be unworthy of our legacy.

Let us approach and appreciate our differences in the way a mature man should. Let us remember that no one point of view, nor any one way of life, has any monopoly of virtue. Quite the contrary: the road to ultimate wisdom lies in comparison, mutual compassion, and understanding. Each of our people, each one individually, has some element of truth, some glimpse of enlightenment to offer to all of us. Therefore when we meet a man with an opinion that is new to us, or a people with a tradition we have not met before, let us look at them with respect and perhaps even with envy, for he and they know something that we do not, he and they have achieved a further step toward wisdom. Then, if we approach the differences between us in this way, respect leads to appreciation, appreciation to understanding, and understanding to affection.

Whether Canada can achieve unity in diversity will depend in the last analysis on our attitude as individuals. Respect for each other, an eagerness to learn, an appreciation of the good in whatever form it takes, a willingness to open our hearts to understanding and affection: all of these are the most contagious of attitudes, and once shown by one person spread like the ripples in a pond to affect actions and outlooks far beyond that person's original ken.

If each of us were an island unto himself, then it might be possible to disclaim responsibility for such attitudes. But we are not islands; each of us is responsible for the future well-being of our community and of our nation.

And on that well-being depends the happiness and prosperity of our children. The need for unity is not something we can put off until tomorrow, for tomorrow may be too late. The need for unity is the most important single problem facing us as a nation today.

For Canada to be a great nation, strong and united, there must be among all Canadians a living and profound sense of the need of one for the other. This friendship supposes, in the first place, a clear and decided devotion to the common good of the nation, but it depends also upon frequent and friendly relations between the different communities, and these relations cannot be friendly unless each community tries to understand the other, to respect its just wants and to complete and aid its needs. Through the experience I have gained across Canada, I am convinced that it is by *knowing* one another that we get to *love* one another.

Not long ago, we received at Government House a large group of teenagers, half French-speaking and half English-speaking. The English-speaking ones had already spent a fortnight up in the Lake Saint-Jean district on an exchange with French-speaking families. The latter had come to reciprocate the visit and were living with English-speaking families in the region of Ottawa. My wife and I were pleased to see how well they appeared to get on. I said suddenly, "You have been together now for quite some time, do you like one another?" The answer was a resounding "Yes." The trouble is we don't see enough of one another ...

The day after tomorrow, I will be receiving twenty-four young people from Newfoundland who are on their way to visit Saskatchewan: they are the vanguard of fourteen thousand who will be taking part in the exchanges this year between the provinces, organized under the Centennial Travel Programme. This is the type of exchange we must have to weld the spiritual unity of our country. I am thrilled by this first exchange.

This is a beginning – but *only* a beginning, I trust – I look forward to many more and even larger contingents. *Now* is the time, not tomorrow, to do this, because tomorrow, as I said before, may be too late.

I am a great optimist about the future – on one condition: we must work together and march forward, all of us, hand in hand in unity. Let us broaden and deepen our horizon. The great hope for Canada is unity through understanding.

Message broadcast on CBC *Television, 1 July 1965*

I SOMETIMES HEAR IT SAID THAT CANADA IS A COUNTRY WITHOUT AN IDEN-
tity. It is an idea, curiously enough, that is only found within Canada –
never abroad. During the time, more than thirty years, that I represented
this country overseas, let me assure you that no identity was better recog-
nized or respected than was the Canadian. Our reputation for fairness, good
judgment, and for understanding without bias was a source of immense
prestige for anyone fortunate enough to represent Canada. We are known
as a people with no axe to grind, without a frontier hate complex. Whenever an international committee was looking for a member, Canadian offi-
cials were in demand. I can vouch that the rest of the world believes that
there *is* a Canadian identity. To people throughout the world, Canada gives
an image of solidarity. In fact there is a Canadian identity which is an "open
sesame" ...

We need to cherish and respect our identity. We must seek those values
in our national life which have won for us so invaluable a name in the
councils of the world. We must concentrate on the development of mutual
trust and understanding, of mutual affection and fraternity; that alone
can make us the united country we must be.

In the development of our national life, let us not always argue about
who is right, but simply *what* is right; what course is fair and just; what
course will lead to the common good. Only as we approach problems in this
honourable way will we be worthy of the esteem with which we are held
abroad. Only as we live up to the image that other nations have of Canada
will the world's faith and trust in us be fulfilled. I am tired of hearing
people around me say and write that we are a lot of rudderless people on
the road to nowhere. We *have* a Canadian identity; we must begin to live
up to the high standard it embodies.

New Year's Message, 1966

THE TWO FOUNDING PEOPLES OF CANADA DID NOT SPRING FROM TWO
separate civilizations, isolated the one from the other, but from the same,
single, Western civilization. The values, the traditions, the beliefs, and the
hopes of English- and French-speaking Canadians have infinitely more in
common of shared characteristics, mutual interests, and bonds of friendship
than they have of differences.

Of course there *are* differences between Canadians of English and French origin, and how fortunate that this is so, for how otherwise could human contacts prove a source of mutual enrichment and inspiration? But when we contemplate these differences let us keep our sense of proportion. If we are one in a spirit of friendship, the differences between us can serve only to enlarge and ennoble each other's thoughts and ideas.

We must therefore approach and appreciate these differences for their real value, as a source of usefulness and enhancement. Each time that we find ourselves considering the contrasts between us in any other light, let us stop at once and take stock of the number of advantages that unity offers our country, and let us remember just how very similar are the ideals and the aspirations of all Canadians.

In reply to address of welcome from the Mayor of Moncton, 16 May 1966
(translation)

THE DIVERSITY OF OUR COUNTRY PROVIDES US WITH THE POTENTIAL FOR lives of richness and variety, on condition that we develop the mutual respect and understanding so essential if we are to live in harmony and happiness. Each of us has some vital contribution to make to our country, a contribution which is distinctive. If we all thought alike, none of us would think very much. Let us rejoice in our different points of view and ways of doing things, for every one of us can learn something of value from each of our brothers.

Message for the Second Annual International Week, Lethbridge Junior
College, Lethbridge, January 1967

WHAT HAVE WE DONE IN OUR FIRST ONE HUNDRED YEARS SINCE CONFEDERAtion? Our material achievements have been dramatic. Faced with the challenge of forging the physical unity from the vast sprawling expanses of 1867, we built, by hard work and enterprise, the railways, the highways, the shipping and air services that conquered the barriers of distance. Our population has grown from less than four to more than twenty million. The total value of goods and services produced in our country has increased twenty-five-fold.

We can be proud of these material accomplishments, because they were achieved by hard work and intelligence. We should be proud as well, and especially, of our progress in the intellectual and spiritual sense. This first century has seen Canada emerge from a group of provinces into an independent and respected world power. We have made a vital contribution in two wars to the cause of freedom and justice, and have played a role in the preservation of peace.

To be aware of our accomplishments, we all must know our history. Confederation is one hundred years old, but the settlement of Canada dates back over three and one-half centuries, during most of which the two founding peoples, first the French and then the British, then both together, with people of other origins, have coexisted and co-operated. We must learn the lessons of our past, lessons of bravery and brotherhood, lessons of love and service to one another and to our country. Understanding our nation's story will make us nobler and wiser persons.

Perhaps we have not done everything which we should have done or would like to have done, but to emphasize now our quarrels and our shortcomings leads only to bitterness best forgotten. The fact remains that what we have accomplished has been done working *together*, perhaps not always in complete understanding. But let us remember and cherish that which is creative in our history.

The measure of our unity has been the measure of our success and this, I believe, will be more important in the centuries to come, because our unity is a lesson that may help other nations in these troublous times of conflict.

If we imagine that we can now go our separate ways within our country, if we think that selfish interests can now take precedence over the national good, if we exaggerate our differences or revel in contention, if we do any of these things, we will promote our own destruction. As a nation divided we could not attain the great destiny to which God has called us. Not only would further progress be impossible, we would lose the gains that we have made in the past.

But if we remain united, if we seek first and always the greater good, if we cherish, not the digressions which divide us, but the major bonds of shared heritage and common values which unite us, if we do these things, then we can look forward to a future which will make the progress of this century seem pale by comparison.

The resolution which the Canadian nation must now propose for 1967, and for the century to come, is the unity of our country. The road to unity is the road of love: love of one's country and faith in its future will give new direction and purpose to our lives, lift us above our domestic quarrels, and unite us in dedication to the common good.

To fulfil the promise with which Providence has endowed us, unity is essential. We owe it to the world, as well, because no lesson is more badly needed than the one our unity can supply, the lesson that diversity need not be cause for conflict but, on the contrary, may lead to richer and nobler living. We should make every effort to prove to other nations that they too can find the way out of the misunderstandings which engender unhappiness.

Each of us can make his own contribution to our country's unity. Let us lift our thoughts from selfishness to the good of the whole nation. May I repeat what I have so often said. We are ten provinces. I am proud of each one of them, proud of their inhabitants, but not always happy that the boundaries between the provinces at times look more like barriers than happy meeting-places. Let us open the windows and the doors of the provinces. Let us look over the walls and see what is on the other side. Let us *know* one another; *that* will lead to understanding. I want to be known abroad and at home as a Canadian, not only as a citizen of one of the provinces.

I pray God that we may all go forward hand in hand. We can't run the risk of this great country falling into pieces.

I can find no better words to express my thoughts than those of a Centennial Anthem written for the Canadian Interfaith Council which embraces thirty-two religious groups in Canada:

> Lead us to walk the ways that love has always taken,
> Guide us, O God of Love, and we will shape a spirit
> Worthy a nation reaching for her destiny.
> So may we show the world a vision of Thy goodness,
> Our dream of Man to which all men may yet awaken
> And share the glory still with Thee.

New Year's Message, 1967

Aspects of National Life: Democracy

HOW OFTEN WE HEAR THAT THERE IS TOO MUCH TALK AND NOT ENOUGH action in some parliaments. Perhaps that's true, but what's wrong with that? The very word "parliament" means talk, argument, discussion – free speech instead of compulsion without a hearing.

I much prefer too much talk by members of parliament and a decision based on an exchange of ideas to the silence that shrouds the evil designs of tyranny.

Through the ages there have been countless tryants; one by one, time has disposed of them. Sooner or later the will of the people triumphed. At times I wonder why. It makes one feel that there must be something profound in the saying *vox populi vox Dei*. Is it part of a Providential plan that, in the end, democracy prevail? Is it that, inherent in the people, there is a natural authority which asserts itself and overrides other considerations?

To believe in democracy means that we are convinced that human nature is capable of rising to the heights that justice and fraternity require to ensure the dignity of man. No means of political self-expression less than democracy can fulfil our craving as rational and compassionate beings ...

§ I congratulate you on the nobility of your mission, and the opportunity that is yours to make known the virtues of democracy. Democracy is built on fundamental concepts of liberty and equality, on mutual respect as opposed to selfish interest, on mutual co-operation instead of arbitrary dictation. To have faith in democracy means to recognize both the rights and the dignity of man.

Playing as they do a key role in the evolution of our contemporary society, the parliaments of our countries must remain faithful to the principles which led to the creation of democracy. But this does not mean that parliament should be either a static or rigid institution, because without change there can be no really viable democracy. Nor can parliaments prosper without the active participation of all the peoples of our nations. The corollary of this fact is that the citizens of all countries must achieve a new awareness of their civic responsibility. To do so is a vital prerequisite for the survival of democracy.

We must never forget that we share common aspirations and common interests, that there is much that unites us one with another. Such unity implies mutual responsibilities, and we cannot assume these vital responsibilities without the help and sustenance afforded by the parliamentary system. Such a system alone can guarantee the freedom of expression of the individual and promote mutual respect for the opinions of others.§

Notes for remarks for the Inaugural Address at the Fifty-Fourth Annual Conference of the Inter-Parliamentary Union, Ottawa, 8 September 1965

PARLIAMENTARY GOVERNMENT IS THE MOST SUCCESSFUL METHOD OF democracy which has, as yet, been achieved. I do not say that it is without its imperfections. It may well be, in our respective nations, that some of our citizens are more qualified than others to choose the leaders of their country. But each one of our citizens has a comparable ability to suffer when the choice is poorly made, and so to each should be given the alternative of rejecting or maintaining the government of the day. This single axiom, embodying as it does the essence of human justice and individual dignity, is the most cogent argument in favour of democracy. A second one is that man has been created by God a free person, with a free will and the power to choose for himself. If this be so, then democracy is the only political expression in which these rights can be respected. Any dictatorship, by definition, is a denial of freedoms ...

Democracy is the most nearly ideal philosophy of politics, and its implementation has been proven to be best entrusted to a parliamentary system. This trust leaves parliament vulnerable to all sorts of criticism. Perhaps, for example, some of your parliaments as well as ours have been accused of too much discussion and too little action. Do we need to overworry about this criticism? So long as our discussions carry out a constructive exchange of ideas, there is not sufficient reason for doubting the efficiency of our parliamentary system. Constructive discussion is a vital part of parliament. I do not have to remind you that to *keep* discussion constructive is a difficult and delicate task. Therein lies a challenge to the parliamentary system. I have said that parliament is the best form of political organization, but although it *is* the best, it is also the most difficult, in

§Translated from the French.

that it gives freedom of expression to everyone irrespective of his ability.

It has been said that "democracy is based upon the conviction that there are extraordinary possibilities in ordinary people." As the expression of democracy, parliament places a corresponding faith in its individual members. As perhaps with few other people, you are asked constantly to place the good of your country before your own personal ambitions, and the wishes of your constituents before your own personal feelings. Your responsibilities are great, but so also are your opportunities of service, service to a cause greater than yourselves, the cause of the freedom and integrity of your country – you are the guardians of a sacred trust.

We have all witnessed the tragedies which occur when a parliament betrays this trust. You will have read that it was forces outside parliament that overthrew the parliament of such and such a country, or that factors beyond the control of parliament led to its own extinction. I suggest to you that this is not always so. If a parliament fails to retain its leadership of a nation, the cause of that failure lies principally among the parliamentarians themselves. If parliament functions as it should, the faith and the confidence it should generate in the people it serves will be stronger than a coup d'état could hope to overcome.

However, if parliament begins to forget its function as defender of its people's faith, if the erosion of self-seeking ambitions, or greed, or cynicism begins to set in among its members, if individual parliamentarians start to consider their position just an occupation and not a trust, if a party believes more in obstruction than construction, more in vilification than co-operation, more in demagoguery than reason, more in emotion than justice, then the cancer of corruption will grow until it consumes not only parliament but the country as well.

On opening the Twelfth General Commonwealth Parliamentary Conference, Ottawa, 28 September 1966

Aspects of National Life: The Commonwealth

I AM SURE I DO NOT NEED TO POINT OUT TO YOU THE DISTINGUISHING aspects of the Commonwealth – mutual respect, friendly discussion, a tradition of justice, freedom, and fair play, an appreciation of education, economic progress, and social equality. I think one of the most important of them has been the spirit of compromise and the virtue of flexibility. This flexibility has meant a wide diversity in the forms of government and in the separate progress towards independence of the different members of the Commonwealth.

You are all aware of the initiatives taken by Canadian representatives at the imperial conferences held between 1926 and 1930, resulting, as they did, in the changes embodied in the Statute of Westminster. It has been said more than once that the present conception of the Commonwealth owes more to Canadian thinking and Canadian influence than to any other sources. It is true that from the beginning we have wanted to have the best of both possible worlds, by which I mean that we have wanted complete independence but we have earnestly wished to retain our ties with Commonwealth countries across the seas.

It goes without saying that Canada's dual heritage had much to do with shaping our attitude towards the Commonwealth. The diversity of our origins tended to make us look outwards, while within our country it developed within us a special capacity to help evolve strength from diversity, and it was this strength from diversity which turned out to be the nature of the evolving Commonwealth relation.

That is why I think it fair to say that from the beginning Canada's conception of the Commonwealth proved to be forward looking. I think it was probably the only conception which could, in the end, have accommodated the non-British peoples of the Commonwealth, who, today, comprise the vast majority of its members ...

The Commonwealth today, therefore, is something truly unique in the annals of political history. If we were pressed to define it, I think we could best call it a partnership, a partnership based on a measure of common historical recollection and a framework of common values and institutions, but especially upon a willingness to consult and to co-operate on a basis of mutual confidence. We now enjoy a partnership of nations in which people of all origins may take justifiable pride ...

The strength of the Comonwealth lies far from the world of atom bombs and defence groups and bayonets. It lies in its moral influence in world affairs, and this influence is tremendous and growing all the time. The Commonwealth has developed a community sense despite its differences in language, race, tradition, and religion ... [It] has created a new tradition of compromise, mutual respect, and co-operation.

It is the extent to which everyone of us shows these qualities in our own personal approach to Commonwealth questions that will determine the future strength and glory of this institution. Only through the combined efforts of Commonwealth members towards greater understanding will the Commonwealth realize its full potential as a force for creative good in this troubled world. Only as we study and learn more of our fellow Commonwealth members can we expect to know and understand them. Only as we understand them can we realize that their hopes and aspirations are close to, if not identical with, our own. Only as we realize the universality of human brotherhood and compassion can we forge the Commonwealth into the creative force it must be. It is up to us to fulfil the privilege we have been given in being members of the Commonwealth. It is up to us to accept the trust that has been bestowed upon us in the Commonwealth tradition and to fulfil this trust for the betterment of all mankind.

Notes for remarks at the Royal Commonwealth Society Dinner, Montreal,
12 May 1965

Aspects of National Life: The Governor-General

IN MANY WAYS GOVERNMENT HOUSE PERSONIFIES THE NATION. OFTEN IT is the only Canadian home which some foreign visitors come to know. Its hospitality, of course, is not confined to foreign visitors; Canadians from all walks of life are welcomed as well.

Past governors-general, in their quiet way, have exercised an influence on the destiny of the Canadian nation, providing, as they have, wise advice outside of politics and removed from the emotions of day-to-day partisan involvement.

Government House serves on occasion as a neutral meeting-ground, a setting where disciples of opposing interests can reconcile and compromise. This neutrality is possible only because the governor-general is removed from political controversy and, representing as he does the monarchy, provides the continuity and sense of permanence so valuable in the transient politics of a democracy.

From Foreword to Rideau-Hall – An Illustrated History of Government House, Ottawa, Victorian and Edwardian Times, *by R. H. Hubbard, 28 November 1966*

Aspects of National Life: The Civil Service

THE CANADIAN PUBLIC SERVICE HAS HAD A LONG AND SOMETIMES PAINFUL development to its present degree of excellence. In the distant past, a publication called *Canadian Monthly,* published in November 1876, defined the requirements for entering government employment as: "the free exercise of a glib tongue, deftness in political canvassing, and unscrupulousness in everything," and even an official report of the Commission on the Public Service, 1880, felt constrained to say that the Service was "A refuge for people who, by reason of their indolence or lack of intelligence, could not succeed in other employment" ...

Recently, I came across this translation of some precepts laid down some thousands of years ago for the Egyptian Civil Service: "Be courteous and tactful as well as honest and diligent. All your doings are publicly known, and must therefore be beyond complaint or criticism. Be absolutely impartial. Always give a reason for refusing a plea; complainants like a kindly hearing even more than a successful plea. Preserve dignity but avoid inspiring fear. Be an artist in words, that you may be strong for the tongue is a sword ..."

Besides proving that, as the man said, a circular memorandum is the nearest thing we have to immortality in this world, these words of advice across the centuries are worth remembering for themselves. They emphasize that, though he may be more skilled, the public servant of today shares with his predecessors the one great purpose of serving the public, faithfully and to the very best of his ability.

Not long ago I read of someone objecting to the designation "public *servant.*" It was, he said, demeaning. I disagree with him. I know of no more noble occupation than service, and no higher calling than the service of the public. As the name of your organization makes clear, it is a profession. It is not an interlude for amateurs or a school for the money-grubbing, any more than it is an amusement for the unambitious or a haven for the unable. It is, above all else, not a business. Its inspiration and cause have nothing to do with the making of money but are – and must always be – wholly concerned with the rendering of an essential service not only to the state but to each citizen ...

It has been said, and history has proved, that "As soon as public service ceases to be the chief business of the citizens, and they would rather serve with their money than with their persons, the state is not far from its fall." We teach people to obey the law, pay their taxes. If we are not to have them feel that their responsibilties have been discharged by money payment, we must also lead them to serve with their persons.

Notes for remarks at a dinner of the Professional Institute of the Public Service of Canada, Ottawa, 13 March 1964

Aspects of National Life: The Armed Forces

IT WOULD BE WRONG TO BELIEVE THAT THE ARMY HAS A REASON FOR existence only in time of war. Surely no one is more aware of the inestimable value of *peace* than he who has experienced at first hand the full horrors of war.

Within a country the army provides a last resort in the guarantee of public order. On the international plane, the army remains the primary deterrent of aggression, and in our present times, peace-keeping operations have offered yet another and valuable role for it to perform. Canada's will for peace throughout the world has been given substance by our willingness to send peace-keeping forces wherever local crises threaten to burst into conflagration.

When the Korean challenge presented itself, three battalions from this regiment were soon in the front line of battle. In 1953, within the framework of the obligations Canada assumed in Nato for the over-all defence of Europe, yet another battalion was sent to Germany. Again today the Royal Twenty-Second is in the thick of things, and its First Battalion is in Cyprus engaged in a most difficult operation in the service of peace.

Military life, forged as it is from discipline and comradeship, provides a training in citizenship and encourages a sense of civic responsibility, and this sense of responsibility forms the backbone of our society. We should never underestimate the contribution a soldier makes as a citizen.

The qualities which make courageous soldiers are the same ones needed to guarantee the development of our country. Discipline, tenacity, and moral strength, these are the qualities we need if we are to realize the vast potential of our natural and human resources.

In a few days Her Majesty the Queen will inaugurate the memorial to the regiment at the Citadel in Quebec. Within this memorial will be found the Book of Remembrance in which are inscribed the names of the 1450 men from this regiment who died on the field of honour. Beside this Book of Remembrance an everlasting flame will burn in memory of their sacrifice.

Today, a half century afterwards, we think of those who chose the road of combat, of danger and suffering, and, in too many cases, of death – the road which leads a nation to greatness. We think of those who died on the field of honour, and the words of Lacordaire spring to mind: "Oh Lord, will you not bestow a special grace upon those brave souls who arrive before You in the folds of their country's flag."

At the Fiftieth Anniversary of the Royal Twenty-Second Regiment, Montreal, 26 September 1964 (translation)

THE YOUNG SOLDIER, SAILOR, OR AIRMAN WHO RETURNS TO CIVILIAN LIFE after a time in the armed forces more often than not returns as a much more mature and self-controlled person than when he enlisted. In this respect, the armed forces contribute handsomely to the community. The contribution is further increased by anything that the former officer or enlisted man may do to bring out the traits of leadership or the sense of responsibility instilled by military training. Here again the community is substantially enriched. In both cases it is as a result of what is basically an educational process ...

We are a free people. The overpowering strength of a free people is the readiness voluntarily to defend not merely themselves, not only their allies, but the very democratic principles they cherish; and this against attack or corrosion, from without or from within ...

Those of us who have known war are very mindful of its real meaning. The experience and lessons of days gone by are heavily impressed upon our minds. They influence our appreciation of current events. Civil liberty, the rights and duties of citizenship, the opportunities of nationhood – these and many related subjects have a particular, unforgettable quality in the minds of men who have fought for them ...

I have frequently remarked to young people that each time a soldier has given his life on the field of battle, he has registered, as absolutely as it is possible to register, his conviction that the values and ideals of our civilization are worth while. He has passed to the living, and particularly to the young, the responsibility for maintaining that civilization and serving its values and ideals.

The sense of service, self-discipline, and good citizenship must be inculcated into young people. We cannot expect our schools and churches to do this vital work alone. We must help them and it seems to me that a military institute is especially well placed, well equipped, and – indeed – particularly charged with providing this help.

Our Service traditions and ideals are meaningful only in the larger context of our national purpose. Men who pretend to know something about fighting are especially responsible for voicing the message and executing the will of those who, going abroad to fight, have not returned.

Our military tradition is not one of aggression but of defence. Its glory is not war itself but what victory in war has preserved. The dedication of our officer corps – past, present, and future – is to peace and to civilization, to happiness and prosperity among men. For the officer and former officer there is, in Canada, a noble role of leadership to fulfil. We have a message to pass on to the youth of this country. We must do all in our power, by speech and by example, to foster and spread a sense of national purpose, the virtue of patriotism, and the ideal of good citizenship.

To the Hamilton and District Officers' Institute, Hamilton,
5 March 1965

THE FLAME WITHIN HIM WHICH ANIMATES THE VOLUNTEER IS THE VERY essence of democracy. Without this flame a large part of all that is dear to us would soon disappear. Our society counts on those who volunteer without restraint for the service of their fellows in the spirit of duty and loyalty. If this truth applies to all types of activity and to every profession, surely it applies more imperatively to the armed forces of our country.

§ The militia is the reinforcement of the regular army ... The volunteer reserves of a trained citizenry have other major roles also. One is to represent the armed forces in the community and to provide a link between soldier and civilian which is more than ever necessary in days of international tension. This is no mean task and requires a sense of purpose and a standard of deportment of the highest order.

Another, and most important function of the militia is as a training ground in the manly arts of citizenship, and this pursuit I cannot too highly recommend. For those who teach and those who learn, ... there are dividends not only personal, but national. A country needs not only soldiers, but the best qualities of the best soldiers. So it is that we look to the militia ... to provide men trained to courage and discipline in the pursuit of the public interest.§

At the ceremonial parade at the Drill Hall, Ottawa, in connection with the change of command of the Governor-General's Foot Guards,

12 February 1965

YOU OF THE ROYAL TWENTY-SECOND REGIMENT AND THOSE WHO HAVE preceded you have understood that "to love one's country" means as well to be continually ready to defend it. You are not simply "another" regiment, even less "a regiment like the rest of them" – you incarnate the soul of people, the French-Canadian people ... On your shoulders rests the responsibility of helping to make the French-Canadian people known to the rest of Canada, and at the same time of interpreting to French Canadians the thoughts and actions of our fellow-citizens of other origins. Canadian unity provides the only hope for Canada's future, and you can contribute to this unity in helping to develop mutual understanding and greater knowledge among the various people of this country.

At Camp Valcartier, 19 October 1966 (translation)

§Translated from the French.

Aspects of National Life: Civic Spirit

CIVIC SPIRIT I WOULD DEFINE AS THE SEEKING OF THE COMMON GOOD IN
our daily lives. One of the great thinkers of our age has warned us that
"participation in political life is the natural expression of love of one's
fellows because such love should inspire each citizen to contribute as much
as he can to the wellbeing of his own country. We must create a climate of
public opinion which, without searching for scandal, nonetheless exposes
with candor and courage those persons and activities which run counter
to the law or to the institutions of justice, or are trying to hide the truth."
There you have the two key components of civic spirit – truth and justice.

At Laurentian University, Sudbury, 27 October 1961 (translation)

THE ESSENCE OF GOOD CITIZENSHIP IS THE ACCEPTANCE OF RESPONSI-
bility; ... every citizen is under bond not only for himself and his family,
but for his community and his country. Citizenship is not something for
passive minds. The lonely person who stands on the side lines watching and
criticizing is no citizen but a passer-by, for citizenship demands participation, involvement, and contribution. No man can lead a life of significance
if he lives in isolation.

*At sod-turning ceremony for the St. John Branch of the University of New
Brunswick, 17 May 1966*

ONE OF OUR GREATEST NEEDS TODAY IS FOR A WIDESPREAD AND WIDE-AWAKE
civic spirit. Such a spirit might be based upon public opinion, formed by
balanced thinking and respect for truth. Students today may feel that an
idea of this sort is a bit old-fashioned, at a time when the "angry young
man" has achieved a certain notoriety. They may argue that the period of
university training is the ideal moment for attacking accepted views. They
may consider it the opportunity par excellence for paradox and criticism.
To them I would say – go on, be angry, lose your tempers, overthrow the
ancient idols! But let your anger issue into effective action, don't allow it to
degenerate into sterile despair. Try to outdo the older generations. Take
the risk to show your mettle and to do better than we have done. Run for

office, and let no doubts about your careers deter you from bold incursions into public business.

At Convocation, St. Joseph's University, Moncton, 14 May 1961

THE LEADERS OF A PROFESSION ARE THOSE WHO FASHION ITS GREATNESS. To their example of service and integrity, even more than to their accomplishments, people look for the criteria of ethical and moral conduct that will guide other members of the calling and often the community as well. In the public and the civil service, this pervasive influence of leaders is the greater because every citizen is and must always be directly involved in the process of government. The standards of the leaders are, therefore, of crucial importance to the healthy survival of the entire community.

At the presentation of the Vanier Medal of the Institute of Public Administration of Canada to Mr. Arnold Heeney, at Government House,
31 January 1964

IT IS ... NO EXAGGERATION TO SAY THAT A NATION'S WELL-BEING DEPENDS in large measure on the civic spirit of its citizens. If citizens are aware of their responsibilities to their city, alert for ways to fulfil and implement their duties, scrupulous in their integrity, and compassionate in their generosity, both the city and the country can be assured of greatness.

On opening the new City Hall, Toronto, 13 September 1965

THE MUNICIPALITY IS THE BASIC BUILDING BLOCK OF NATIONAL GOVERNment. Indeed, it is at the municipal level that the first steps must be taken in the creation of both civic and national institutions. The size of the municipality is such that each citizen does not feel submerged. It is at this level that our citizens can first develop those qualities of application, initiative, and integrity which can develop into a sense of civic responsibility common to our entire nation. Whatever, therefore, may be the size of the community, it still possesses singular importance, for it remains the foundation of organized society.

At Sherbrooke, 10 September 1962 (translation)

OUR SOCIETY IS BECOMING DAILY MORE SOPHISTICATED, MORE SELF-AWARE, more self-assertive. The tragedy of our time is that men's minds and spirits have not kept pace with the development of our technology and speed of living on the one side, and our new pride and social independence on the other. If we are to forestall the degeneration and perhaps even the disintegration of our society, we must have as leaders ... the type of man who is dedicated to the development, not of his own vanity and power, but of service to his community, and the enhancement of its welfare.

On the national level, this means that we must have men aware of the blessings that God has given our country and determined to lead it along paths worthy of such endowments. Breadth of vision is a strong point for greatness both in a man and in a country, vision based on solid conviction, determination to succeed, and the wisdom of experience.

At the Seventieth Anniversary Dinner, Loyola College, Montreal,
25 March 1966

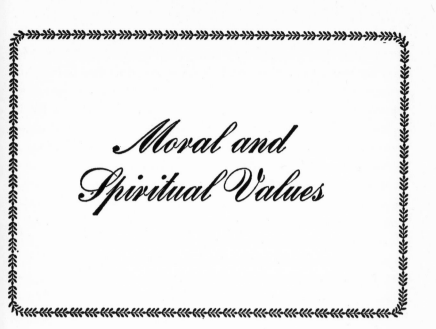

Moral and Spiritual Values

I BELIEVE THAT THERE IS A SPIRITUAL POWER WHICH FINALLY DRAWS TO-
gether the people of a nation. Their unity is founded on love. Such love has
nothing selfish about it, for it is the non-possessive love of friendship. By
rational means, it seeks the good of fellow-men. It finds expression in good
citizenship, in respect for law and the rights of others, and supremely in the
sacrifice of those who have given their lives for the benefit of their brethren.

If we are to take this deep and mature approach to the question of our
common life as one people I believe that we have to evolve spiritually.
Living things appear to have evolved from the individual cell to the complete human being. Machines have developed from the flint instrument to
the atomic reactor. Meanwhile how much advance has been made by will-
power, intellect, and memory considered together? It seems that the human
personality as a whole has to make up a lot of leeway simply to keep pace
with the achievements of its more gifted exponents.

Material progress alone I believe to be sterile and sometimes self-defeat-
ing. It should be considered as a means and not as an end in itself. When

this distinction is forgotten the dignity of man usually suffers, and more often than not he is stripped of his natural rights. Science and technology, those two main props of material progress, have been described as wild horses which only human thought can control. Civilization is the aim of our manner of living, culture the object of our pattern of thought. To the former we should strive to give meaning, to the latter depth. If we can succeed in this double effort we shall improve the quality of our lives, we shall maintain our self-respect and keep ourselves distinct as individuals and as Canadians. By mental effort we can avoid the loss of identity; the person will triumph over the nameless mass.

By evolving spiritually, by becoming more fully conscious of our situation, we can gain the ability to cope with the problems that beset us. What guarantee is there, though, that we will give the right answers to the questions we have been able to pin-point and analyse? To my mind the best hope of avoiding grave errors lies in improving the quality of our human capital. How can this be done? – only by a return to morality. Such a return would achieve more than the most successful application of political or economic theory.

At present vice and crime are accepted as a part of life and often glamourized by authors and entertainers. There exists a cult of success – and who hasn't heard of the perfect murder? We have come dangerously near to an acceptance of the doctrine that the end justifies the means. In such circumstances it is hardly surprising that the young have difficulty in recognizing right and wrong – hence their dismay and even despair. Our angry young men and our juvenile delinquents are not just a plague sent to try their virtuous parents; they are a direct consequence of the moral climate for which we are responsible. If we base morality on sound values which we are not ashamed to proclaim, then there is little cause for fear. This way lies the road to maturity.

At a luncheon of the Empire Club, Toronto, 9 February 1961

SPIRIT, I BELIEVE, WILL BE ESSENTIAL IN CONSTRUCTIVE WORK FOR YOUTH. But what is this rather nebulous conception of Spirit? May I perhaps be allowed to define it as that which lends dignity to man, enabling him to transcend his limitations. Many of us lead tidy lives, with steady jobs, a well-ordered routine, and little stimulus to additional activity. Yet we admire the spirit of those who tamed the wilderness, who converted the heathens, or who adventured into the unknown realms of science.

Nevertheless, it is easy to fall into effortless, materialistic ways. Mere numbers and size impress us by their impact. The immensity of geological time and cosmic space leave us bewildered, and disinclined to ask further questions. There is much to be done to help the apathetic body by awakening its soul. We must find our souls in order to redress the disproportion of our physical achievements. For in the field of science, to put it colloquially, we have got above ourselves. Some of our discoveries have surprised even the discoverers. Lethal weapons of a frightening character exist, without their being any evidence, on the spiritual side, that man has reached the state of, at all times, loving his neighbour. We are able to probe the outer reaches of space while we remain unable to see into the inner recesses of man's mind. We devote much time and energy to mastering the forces around us, but the forces within still go, in large measure, undeveloped.

Now is the time to study the eternal values and the betterment and the direction of man, rather than his destruction. Otherwise instead of shaping their own destiny men will lose control and become the servants of their creatures. The new forces have changed everything except our way of thought and life. There is not much hope if we do not make serious attempts to direct these forces into channels of goodwill and peace.

I am no pessimist but I would ask: what does this uncertain world need, when science has missiled up, leaving ethics and morals earthbound? The answer is simple – a soul. Our best hope of controlling otherwise purposeless and undisciplined movement is to base our actions upon a spirit of love and faith.

Faith in what? Faith in God, who has made and ordained heaven and earth. Am I something out of the Middle Ages to speak thus? If so, I am in very good company, a company of men of science, of physicists, and doctors. One of the latter, chairman of a department of the New York University College of Medicine, recently declared that he could not practise the rehabilitation of the physically handicapped if he did not believe in God and in prayer. We are faced with problems so grave, so tragic, so cosmic that we shall not be able to cope with them if we have recourse to human means and methods alone.

101

I have spoken to you of prayer and spiritual values. Why? Because I believe we must shape our lives on moral standards, personal as well as public,
higher than those existing today. Let us begin to associate prayer with
power, faith with fire, charity with clear, swift action. May these spiritual
shafts shatter the clouds of doubt and fear, and guide us upon our Pilgrim's
Progress.

From an address to the Men's Canadian Club of Vancouver, 24 May 1960

TODAY MATERIAL THINGS HAVE SUCH A POWER OF ATTRACTION FOR THE
minds of men that the standard of living sometimes seems more important
than the purpose of life. So much so that just as in the days of St. Paul
altars may sometimes be seen dedicated to the unknown God. You, on the
other hand, assert the importance of spiritual values. Now the idea of value
necessarily implies choice. It involves an act of will. The values you carry
within you are capable therefore of being your guide of conduct, a compass to pilot you through life.

Of all the attributes of the spirit, the greatest is love. By this power the
Good Shepherd and his flock know each other. From him we have the two
great commandments of love. Let us not be tempted to restrict these commandments to a narrow view of charity – namely love of one's neighbour
only after providing for oneself. Charity in the Judaic tradition embraces
justice, and this according to Plato is the virtue by which a man has and
does all that rightly belongs to him. This activity of the whole man is the
test of love. May your lives therefore be founded on love, and hallowed by
prayer which is love's expression.

From an address to Emmanuel College, Saskatoon, 4 May 1960

HUMAN RELATIONS DEPEND FOR THEIR EFFECTIVENESS UPON UNDERSTAND-
ing. It may be said that a man is free to the extent that he understands.
Nevertheless a man's understanding of a given situation may be logically
and intellectually correct, yet totally ineffective, because lacking in sympathy. It is a human characteristic that we desire not only to be loved, but
to be loved in the way we wish. Conversely, many of us are willing to love

others, but only in the way we wish to love them. The practical result of this is that in all areas of disagreement where opinions are strongly held, it is necessary to understand the other man's belief as he understands it himself. We have not only to see the other fellow's point of view, but, as it were, to feel it too.

At the annual dinner of the Canadian Press, Royal York Hotel, Toronto, 19 April 1961

NO MAN CAN BE SATISFIED WITH A PURELY INDIVIDUALIST PHILOSOPHY IF he seeks a whole and happy life. Any man worthy to be called a man must hold to an ideal or a sense of purpose in life to which he clings above all else – above wealth, above professional success – an ideal in short which gives real value to his life, which forms an underlying unity through all his various activities, which gives to each of his accomplishments their true significance. A man who holds to a profound ideal has at the same time the courageous breadth of spirit necessary to achieve his goal. He is able to turn even the difficulties he meets to his profit. Obstacles in his path become merely challenges which push him to new heights of accomplishment. The depths of his being are broad and vital enough for him to emerge from the crises of life strengthened and ennobled. Great minds and spirits are capable of giving themselves in quest of a goal which is greater than they, in quest of an ideal to which they can sacrifice everything. They are capable, too, of inspiring others to follow in their wake and to enliven in those who follow a sense of hope and genuine enthusiasm.

At a social welfare dinner, Montreal, 15 February 1962 (translation)

TODAY, AS NEVER BEFORE, EVERYONE IS OUR NEIGHBOUR. A NEIGHBOUR IS not only the person who lives next door, or on the same street, or even in the same city or country – nowadays neighbours are everywhere and anywhere. He whose voice and image can be brought into our homes by the miracles of modern science is our neighbour.

Message for Boy Scout Week, 1963

THE APPLICATION OF THE GOSPEL TO SOCIAL ACTION IS THE CALLING OF ALL Christians and, it would seem to me, co-operation in this visible work of love the most important – if also the most rudimentary – expression of the oecumenical spirit. It is a way that requires neither domination nor effacement. It requires only working together in faith, in hope, and in love.

It is a stock phrase of churchmen everywhere that, in our individual lives and activities, we should count our blessings. Perhaps we might do well among the various confessions to count the blessings we hold in common. The things that unite us are many and sacred, as exemplified in the life and works of Christ. And, of course, the great link that binds us to God and to our fellow man is prayer. Yes, my friends, let us pray for one another.

At a meeting of the Executive of the General Council of the
United Church of Canada, United Church House, Toronto,
5 November 1963

RESPECT FOR ALL FAITHS AND LOVE FOR ALL MEN ARE THE ONLY FOUNDAtions on which we, and the other nations of the world, can build hope for a future of peace and fraternity for mankind.

Message for Programme of Twelfth Annual Convention of the
United Synagogue Youth, Pacific Northwest Region,
Calgary, 1967

AFFLUENCE IN OUR SOCIETY CAN BE OUR SERVANT OR OUR MASTER. IT CAN make us slaves of pettiness and purposeless living, or by refreshing within us the sources of charity and love, it can make us richer not only materially but richer in heart and mind and spirit as well.

Oh, what a responsibility affluence carries with it – a responsibility to all humanity, to those who are handicapped, to those who are miserable, to those who are hungry.

We must resolve that the principles our forefathers exemplified will guide our work and rekindle within us the force of determination to give worth and meaning to our lives.

New Year's Message, 1966

THERE ARE TWO LAKES – OR SEAS, AS THEY ARE CALLED – IN PALESTINE. One of them accepts the waters of the Jordan, but it gives nothing in return. Its shores are barren and sterile, its waters are stagnant and turgid, nothing can live in or around it – it is called "the Dead Sea." The other sea accepts as well the waters of the Jordan, but these it gives back in even greater measure. Around it the countryside is green and happy; its waters teem with life and vitality. Our Lord, when he came to earth, chose to spend his life nearby and loved to visit it. It is called "the Sea of Galilee."

It would be hard to imagine a closer parallel to the two kinds of people which we may chose to be. In so far as we give of ourselves, we live and grow in strength and blessings. In so far as we receive alone, and hoard our blessings and bury our talents, our spirit shrivels up and dies within us. These are old adages, but how hard they seem at times to remember.

Affluence seems to breed a life of affluence, and the richer we become, the more unhappy we seem to be because we haven't even more. Some of you setting out into the confusion of the adult world will wonder what you possibly can give. From a financial point of view, you might be tempted to conclude that your gift will be so small that it would not be worth giving. But serving God with our little is the very way to make it more, and we must never think anything wasted when our God is honoured or men are blessed. We must give according to our means or our means will all too soon shrink to the proportions of our giving.

But in reality, when I speak of gifts, I think much less of money than of attitudes and of qualities. The best thing to give to your enemy is forgiveness; to an opponent, understanding; to a friend, your heart; to yourself, respect; and to all men, your love. Every gift, no matter how small, is in reality great if it is given with affection.

Probably never will you find again such flowering of your God-given instincts for generosity and idealism as you feel when you are young. Your stage in life is the most nearly perfect combination of intelligence and the instinct to give of yourself. You must not let it pass, ignored or under-valued. Now is the time when you must weigh and appreciate the blessings you have been given and the inheritance you have been granted. Now is the time when you must resolve to use the talents you have been given to their maximum advantage in the service of God and of your fellows. You must base your resolution on the solid rock of spiritual conviction so that your dedication to service will weather whatever storms of cynicism and indifference you are liable to meet. Only in so far as you do so will you learn the true purpose of living and will your lives fill up with the spirit of joy and freedom. Only as all Canadians of your age do so can our country hope to realize the greatness and nobility that its endowments have offered it.

At Saint Mary's University, Halifax,

13 May 1966

ONLY AS WE DEVELOP AN AWARENESS OF THE NEEDS AND FEELINGS OF others can we hope to rise to real stature and spiritual manhood. Our country as a whole will be great in proportion to the compassion its citizens show for each other. Let us remember that just as none of us can be perfectly free until all our people are free, so none of us can be perfectly happy until the well-being of every Canadian is assured.

These are the practical reasons for brotherhood, but I believe that there is a divine reason as well, for there cannot be a brotherhood of man without the fatherhood of God. Let each of us, of whatever faith, look to our spiritual well-springs and we will discover that divine instinct for brotherhood which is the source of all justice and liberty and humanity.

Message for Brotherhood Week, 19–26 February 1967, sponsored by the Canadian Council of Christians and Jews

IN THIS MODERN AGE WE SOMETIMES SEEM TO THINK OF MEDICAL TRAINING in terms of its technical complexity, rather than its ultimate purpose in alleviating human suffering. Whether with regard to its acquisition – schools, research centres, wonder drugs, and experiments – or to its practice – hospital buildings, equipment, chemicals, complicated apparatus, and intricate techniques – the emphasis in modern medicine is placed at times on science rather than on the art of curing.

In comparison with even a very few years ago, medical science is very far advanced. The physical plant required for its barest performance is large, complex beyond imagining, and expensive to the same degree. To run this plant and maintain a flow of patients through it is a very difficult task, necessitating many highly specialized skills and an enormous administrative tail.

In the end result we are very fortunate. We can be cured of many diseases once considered fatal. We can be shielded from pain and disfigurement once regarded as unavoidable. For this extension of life and removal of physical suffering the whole patient class is indebted to medical people.

Does our responsibility end here? Is it enough to construct and equip and make available to the sick physical machinery for their treatment? I think not. A hospital is not a factory, impersonally repairing "things," sweeping up broken bits and pieces and sending them out in assembly-line fashion as functioning automata. A hospital is a place for healing people. This is axiomatic, yet how rarely do we remind ourselves of what it means. To heal is to make whole, and as applied to people, wholeness includes not only the body but also the spirit.

Despite all its great discoveries, medical science has yet to discover much about the spirit. That it exists, that people can suffer terribly from a broken spirit, there is no doubt. But what it is and where it is may possibly never be known.

There is no physical illness that does not at some time include also a weakening of the spirit. The treatment of the one necessarily involves concern for the other – but, with this difference, that whereas the physical condition of the body is primarily the domain of the doctor, the care and tending of the spirit is the responsibility of each and every one of us.

I need hardly remind you of the story of the "man who was on his way down from Jerusalem to Jericho." How he "fell in with robbers, who stripped him and beat him, and went off leaving him half dead." We are all familiar with the parable of the Good Samaritan who saw the man there "and took pity at the sight" and "mounted him upon his own beast and brought him to an inn, where he took care of him." We know the story, but how many of us observe its concluding injunction: "Then Jesus said, Go thy way, and do thou likewise"?

The manifestations of a broken spirit are many and varied: loneliness, hopelessness, helplessness, and so on. These are real and terrible afflictions that can reduce the already physically sick just as surely as the most virulent of infections. But it is within the power of all of us to mend the spirit: the remedy is love.

As I have said before, fine equipment, great buildings, neat forms, and advanced techniques are not enough to make a hospital. Within its four walls there must be love. Surely a hospital that dares to found itself upon a religion of love should make every effort to capture within itself this magic quality. For its mercy, its pity, its charity, it should be known by the sick with the same gratitude at heart as storm-tossed sailors know in seeing the beacon at the entrance of a peaceful haven.

In a day of symbolism the significance of identifying hospitals and ambulances by the cross is perhaps overlooked. It should not be. The essence of what medicine is, and always has been, is summed up in the cross ...

One of the greatest of Canadian medical men, Sir William Osler, once said: "Without faith a man can do nothing; with it, all things are possible." On another occasion he said: "Nothing in life is more wonderful than faith – the one great moving force which we can neither weigh in the balance nor test in the crucible." The well of faith is the spirit, and by its encouragement through love we can help in untold ways ...

§ When Jesus delivered his Sermon on the Mount, he saw in one beatific vision all the poor people of the world. And he looked with special compassion not only on those who were poor through social circumstance, but also those made poor through physical inadequacies or suffering. Physical suffering imposes upon its victims a state of continuing illness and even, often, of anguish, which prevent the sufferer from obtaining the rest of which he has the greatest need. Surely it is this incapacitation and this despair which explain the special feelings of love which Jesus had for such sufferers.

The Church has pioneered in setting up numerous institutions of compassion, and even today it seeks continuously to provide what inspiration and guidance it can for such works of loving kindness as these institutions can render, because it feels that such works and institutions form an integral part of the Church's spiritual commission. The fact that the Church still retains responsibility for the operation of many such institutions must surely be one of the glories of the Church in Canada. In our world of the twentieth century, however, it would appear that the administration and operation of these institutions brings new and challenging problems and genuine difficulties.

If these institutions are to remain genuine servants of compassion according to the spirit of the gospel, their activities must meet two requirements. Firstly, if they are to achieve their temporal objective with efficacy and justice, Christian undertakings must prove themselves adequate to meet the challenges of technical competence and administrative demands which they will inevitably meet. But if, secondly, these undertakings are to go forward in the spirit of Christ, their administrative apparatus and their technical resources must remain only a means or a secondary end, indispensable admittedly, but subordinate always to, and inspired by, a higher purpose. These undertakings must be filled with the spirit of compassion for the individual; in other words, they must be filled with a sense of the poverty, of the suffering, and special consideration for all the most unfortunate in life. This is the second but principal requirement of Christian institutions.

Here we are touching on a question of extreme delicacy. The development of modern medical and administrative techniques is not necessarily linked with a corresponding deepening of our sense of compassion, or generous and self-giving dedication to those who suffer. On the contrary, there seems almost to be a certain opposition between these two types of development because they induce us to consider the personality of the sufferer from quite different aspects.

On the one hand, the patient is considered from a purely clinical aspect, one which specifies that his case can and must be given a scientific and technical analysis which will place his illness in a given category of ailment. From this point of view the patient is of interest to our intelligence and to our powers of reasoning. On the other hand, however, the sufferer must also be considered from a purely individual aspect, as a suffering human being who can be understood only through love.

This understanding makes us think immediately of the patient's suffering in a concrete and total perspective. Such suffering, for reasons both accidental and strictly personal, is not necessarily directly proportionate to the degree of the patient's illness. One often finds patients who, according to a medical diagnosis, should be suffering very little or not at all, but ones who we, if we have the heart of a son or a brother, a husband or a wife, know must be undergoing spiritual suffering which is veritable torture, or even physical suffering which, for various reasons, may have escaped the doctor's diagnosis.

No two people experience an identical nature and degree of suffering. Their illnesses or their infirmities may appear similar from a scientific or technical point of view, but the suffering which results from them is always individual, because it depends on a whole range of individual circumstances.

And it is precisely this individual suffering, in so far as it cannot be put into words, and in so far as it cannot be diagnosed scientifically, which calls out kindness from any heart which is really compassionate, and which inspires that heart to seek a remedy for the sufferer.

There is no denying that medicine and surgery have evolved in an admirable fashion, but often they are still unable to restore the sufferer to real, full health, and after having saved him from death, they leave him during long months of convalescence in a state of extreme misery. That is why this very scientific development to which I have paid tribute requires a comparable development of our sense of compassion and loving kindness to allow us to offer understanding and comfort in these new conditions of weakness and suffering.

The technician in us, therefore, must be complemented by elements within us which can make of us instruments of kindness and compassion. We must first of all know how to hear the promptings of our own hearts, and thereby understand the type of suffering which cannot be cured by man, but which can be relieved only through the mercy of God.

Surely it is for these very reasons that all those who concern themselves today with works of compassion have need more than ever before for a deep interior life. Only an interior life can, through the grace of the Holy Spirit, raise above natural limitations the profound sensitivity which is the first and indispensable means for those who would practise loving kindness.

The intellectual and the medical practitioner are naturally receptive to anything which interests them intellectually, or which adds to their scientific understanding, but they are not necessarily drawn by suffering itself. Both the intellectual and the medical worker run the risk of looking unconsciously on their patients merely as interesting subjects from the technical point of view rather than as fellow human beings in distress, fellow human beings who ask for compassion undiluted by scientific curiosity.

Our modern means of classification of disease, much more complex and subtle than previously, increases the risk that the personal aspects of each type of suffering will be neglected. A sensitive and more profound understanding of the subject is all the more vital, to be able to distinguish the individual personality which would otherwise be hidden behind apparent technical similarities among cases of a given type.

To provide an inspiration in the spirit of Christianity for modern therapeutics and to prevent the therapeutic art from becoming merely an abstract science, and as a result, somehow less than human from the patient's point of view, a genuinely supernatural spirituality is essential.

At the present time natural compassion and generosity are not sufficient to guarantee that compassion will automatically be applied in cases of suffering. Nature has been left behind by technology, and technology left to itself can no longer be adequately inspired by love without the help of divine grace. Once natural instincts of love are no longer sufficient, it becomes absolutely vital to seek a love greater than that with which nature endows us, greater in its inspiration, in its application, and in its results.

Is it not, therefore, on the genuinely spiritual plane that Christian hospitals have a magnificent task to undertake? In meeting this challenge, these hospitals will render a true Christian apostolic witness and provide for our modern world a visible incarnation of what divine love can mean for man.§ *Notes for remarks at a banquet of the Catholic Hospital Association of Canada, Chateau Laurier, Ottawa, 18 May 1964*

IS THE CARE OF MENTALLY RETARDED CHILDREN THE CONCERN ONLY OF those most directly affected – their families and guardians? I wonder if I might reflect with you for an instant on the responsibilities that a country has for *all* its citizens. The old, the incurable, the physically handicapped, and the mentally retarded are as much Canadians as any other of us. The difference between a democracy and a tyranny is surely that a democracy believes in the individual value of every human being, whereas tyranny

§Translated from the French.

considers of value only those who are useful in the maintenance of its dictatorship. May I recall a period in modern history (without being more definite) when more than 70,000 mentally retarded children were put to death. The thought of it alone is monstrous.

Democratic countries believe that every human being, even those most handicapped mentally, have a real and profound worth; that every person has been created by God in his image and that every person passes after death into eternal life. Democratic countries believe also that even in those who will never be able to lead normal working lives there exist qualities of the heart in which they can and should find some fulfilment. A country such as Canada which believes in the worth of each human being can *never* consider such persons who are unable to take a full place in the work force of their country as some sort of millstone about its neck – a millstone to be disposed of. How much less should such a country consider hiding such unfortunates behind cold inhuman walls far from the eyes of the rest of the population, as if we should try to forget them. Canada has both an opportunity and a duty to give an example of genuine compassion.

If we, in our speeches and protestations of faith, continue unceasingly to assert the importance of the individual and his ultimate worth, should we not also be willing to prove by positive acts that we believe in what we say? If we honestly believe in the value of each human being, should we not do all in our power to help those who are less gifted or more handicapped than ourselves?

I must confess that I feel ashamed when I realize that all too often our modern civilization preserves the physical life of our mentally handicapped while doing nothing to offer them that human and spiritual fulfilment of which they are capable and to which they have as much claim as we. Too often medical progress in our society has been completely offset by pitiful shortcomings of heart and spirit. It is shocking but true to say that it might be better to let the mentally handicapped die than to let them languish in a purgatory without real existence as human beings. If we keep alive these unfortunates – children or adults – we ought to do all we can to allow the spiritual flowering of which they are capable. I have been told by specialists in this field that there are few human beings so mentally infirm or handicapped who cannot profit *in some way* from affection and love when offered to them.

With these thoughts in mind, I ask you to open your eyes to human suffering, to direct your hearts to those who have not the strength to ask for help. Let us go to them. They are waiting for our care, our affection, and our love. They have already been waiting too long. How can such negligence be anything but a disgrace for a country which claims to be religious? How can it be anything but a disgrace that so often parents feel obliged to hide handicapped children from the public view? When will we wake up to this tragic problem? And I repeat the word tragic, for the figures are there for all to see. I understand that three per cent, more or less, of Canada's children are born with some degree of mental retardation and such unfortunates now total about a half million. We must have schools for the partially handicapped children; we must have workshops for those who cannot work at our usual accelerated tempo. We must have warm and welcoming homes for those who cannot stay with their own families. We must have more laboratories, and more research into the cause and treatment of mental retardation.

I throw out this challenge to all those who believe in the value of the human being – there are hundreds of thousands of inadequately cared for persons who need your scientific knowledge, who have need of your heart, your affection, and your love. Much has been done but how much more remains to do!

I hope you will permit me, in concluding, to consider for an instant the parents of handicapped children. You parents will suffer and you will suffer above all because of a lack of understanding in our society and because of the absence of an adequate number of specialized institutions. I would like you to feel that today there is a great movement being born in support of your children. The whole of Canada must come to the help of those who cannot speak for themselves – such is our responsibility.

But let me say as well that any mother who loves her child, who gives herself to him night and day even though she knows his condition will not improve; a mother who loves without any hope of normal achievement by her child – there, surely, is the most noble love to be found on earth. All the rockets which arc their way towards the moon, all the technical and scientific triumphs, all the economic riches and accomplishments, all these are nothing compared to a human heart which knows how to love and to expect nothing in return.

The world can only be at peace when men will come to realize that the thing of real value to give is the gift of oneself, and, if for some reason they can't do that, the gift of what they have.

Need I say more to stir all Canadians to action?

At the Centennial Crusade Dinner of the Canadian Association for Retarded Children, Toronto, 13 September 1965

THE WORLD HAS BEEN DEVELOPING IN MANY WAYS WITH ASTONISHING speed during recent years, but such development is superficial and material. Measurable quantity has been expanded but not measurable quality. Man has expanded still further that portion of the universe which his technology has conquered, and he has been able to use with greater efficiency the raw materials available to him.

But, as has been observed so wisely, though man may have discovered atomic energy, he did not create it. He simply unleashed natural forces of previously unsuspected power, forces which were imprisoned until man, by means of his technological skill, set them free. The question immediately presents itself: has he set these forces free for good or for evil? The Creator of nature had kept this power hidden, and had used it up to now only in the grand and over-all design of his cosmos. Is its potential still within the compass of rational use by human intelligence, or has it not perhaps now become too enormous even for the most fertile imagination? If we remain so limited in our thinking that we cannot grasp the real purposes of existence, or even, and more particularly, the real values of our own hearts, then do we not run the risk, as we have so often done before, of becoming no longer the masters but rather the slaves of our passions and of our selfishness?

An unassuming Christian who reflects on the present world situation in the light of his faith cannot fail to be seized with misgivings when he considers that man, at the very time when he is pushing back scientific and technological frontiers with almost frantic speed, is ignoring almost to the point of indifference the more contemplative functions of his intelligence. The more he studies the means, the more he forgets the end. In this world of uncertainty and chance, how is he to give expression to a way of life illuminated by faith?

What does our world need now more than anything? It needs a soul and a spirit. It is as if our universe had become some sort of grotesque body, the workings of which were becoming more and more ponderous and confused. At the very time when we need an ever keener sense of real values, we spend our time seeking a merely quantitative common denominator. If we are to counter these ominous trends, we must, whatever the cost, develop with equal celerity our sense of qualitative values. Only the spirit can introduce this qualitative element. Technology by itself is incapable of doing so. That is why I speak of quality and purpose.

But do not think me a pessimist. One often hears the cries of distress of those who long for what they call "the good old times," but I tell you the good times are now. The best time is always the present time, because it alone offers the opportunity for action, because it is ours, because on God's scale it is apocalyptic, a time when the lines between good and evil are clearly drawn, and each one of us must choose his side, a time when there is no longer room for either the coward or the uncommitted.

Notes for remarks when General Vanier received Professor Dale Thomson and seventy-five students from the University of Montreal, 2 March 1967 (translation); General Vanier died only three days later